Early Literacy and the Teacher

Ros Fisher

Hodder & Stoughton
In association with the United Kingdom Reading Association

British Library Cataloguing in Publication Data

Fisher, Ros
  Early literacy and the teacher. – (UKRA)
  I. Title II. Series
  372.401

ISBN 0-340-55331-6

First published 1992

Typeset in Linotron Ehrhardt by
Rowland Phototypesetting Ltd, Bury St Edmunds, Suffolk
Printed in Great Britain for the educational publishing
division of Hodder & Stoughton Ltd, Mill Road, Dunton Green,
Sevenoaks, Kent by St Edmundsbury Press Ltd, Bury St Edmunds, Suffolk.

Contents

Introduction   7

1 The task   11

2 The child   25

3 The teacher   38

4 The National Curriculum   57

5 The teacher as facilitator   72

6 The teacher as model   92

7 The teacher as manager   102

8 The teacher as assessor   116

Conclusion   144

Bibliography   146

Book list   152

Introduction

The development of literacy is considered to be one of the most important elements of schooling by all those concerned: politicians, educationists, parents, teachers and children. Many theories have been postulated and many teaching methods tried – although none have achieved one hundred per cent success. Yet the classroom teacher has to make sense of all these and to make decisions daily about which approaches and materials to use. The aim of this book is to help teachers, and those intending to become teachers, to make sense of the debates and to inform the choices they make about the approaches they employ.

The debate is not a new one. Since the Plowden Report (1967) there has been a tension between rhetoric and reality in the classroom. The placing of the emphasis on learning rather than teaching, while reflecting knowledge about how children learn, left teachers without a positive role when faced with the reality of large classes and often inadequate resources. The way that the debate has tended to polarise between formal and informal styles has not been helpful to the practitioner who has to make sense of it all.

In the particular instance of literacy learning, current views differ about the ways in which reading and writing should be taught. Whilst the National Curriculum is intended to bring more consistency to the learning experiences of children, it is not intended to lay down *how* literacy should be taught. However, views and intentions emerge from the National Curriculum documents and commentaries upon these. The Cox Report (Des, 1988b) and the non-statutory guidelines present a picture of language learning that emphasises the personal and social nature of language while the attainment targets reinforce a more utilitarian view. In addition, the greater emphasis that is now to be placed on the composing of writing and the broadening of assessment procedures of reading should ultimately have an effect on the way that teachers teach. Arguments have polarised in recent years, particularly about the way reading is taught with the result that teachers have become confused about what they are expected to do.

There seem to be three factors in the equation: the task, the child, and the teacher, who is the mediator between the other two. The disagreements arise in the choice of route to achieve the agreed aim of literacy for adulthood. Amongst teachers in schools there is a feeling of concern as to what their role should be within an approach to the teaching of literacy that emphasises the active involvement of the child, encourages comprehension and respects composition efforts. In some ways, such recent developments as the use of 'real books' and 'invented spelling', for instance, have become equated with an indictment of teaching per se. However, the difference lies more in the change of emphasis, from relying on the reading scheme books for the teaching of reading, and the production of correct writing for producing writers, to planned intervention on the part of the teacher.

The argument centres around whether or not reading schemes are essential for learning to read and a questioning of the extent to which actual teaching may or may not be desirable. This is considered by Margaret Donaldson (1989) in her paper *Sense and Sensibility* in which she argues the case for reading schemes and where she concludes that the 'minimal teaching movement' advocates the withholding of 'all systematic help'. However, it seems an over-simplification to equate an extreme interpretation of the role of the teacher and the use of a wide range of reading materials. This emphasis on the materials used, over and above the importance of what the teacher does, has been used in both sides of the debate. In the wake of controversy over the teaching of reading in Bromley, the Director of Education for Kent was reported to have said 'What we want are reading schemes that teach children to read' (*Times Educational Supplement*, 29.1.88). Indeed, Liz Waterland (1985) in her explanation of her approach to the use of non-scheme books reiterates a similar view when she says 'It is the book that will do the teaching' (p. 16). Small wonder that teachers feel marginalised and uncertain about their role.

The purpose of this book is to open out the argument and to consider the role of the teacher in the years leading up to Key Stage One of the National Curriculum. This is not to reduce the importance of the child as an active learner; much has been written about this and reference will be made to various sources for evidence, both for the importance of the child's active involvement in the learning process, but also for the profile of the child as an emerging literate. Neither is it the intention to remove the books that are used in the teaching of reading from the agenda, but the crucial element must be what the teacher expects the child to do with these books and the activities provided through which the child is expected to learn about literacy. Studies of activity in infant and junior classrooms will be reviewed and an attempt made to draw conclusions from these findings as to what makes a successful teacher of literacy.

It is not intended to be unduly prescriptive, but rather to provide teachers with information and discussion that will enable them to choose for themselves. However, it is likely that a feeling of excitement about an approach to literacy in which young children's early efforts at making sense of reading and writing are encouraged and valued will show through. It should not be forgotten, though, that one area where there is a large measure of agreement is in the impact of the quality and conviction of the individual teacher, independent of programme or approach used.

In the first chapter the focus will be on the nature of the task, what is meant by literacy and the ultimate aim of producing literate adults, and an attempt will be made to put some elements of the current debate into perspective. The second chapter will centre on the child, how he/she best learns and what he/she brings to the task. In the third chapter attention will turn to the teacher and some of the recent research into activity in infant and junior classrooms will be reviewed in an attempt to tease out elements that provide success in literacy learning. The National Curriculum will be the focus for the fourth chapter and discussion about the extent to which the ideas considered in the first three chapters are reflected in this. The second part of the book will look further into the role of the teacher as it emerges and various teacher roles will be considered: facilitator; model; manager of learning; and assessor.

No one can provide a blueprint for the perfect classroom and it would be unrealistic to try to do so. It is hoped, however, that the review of both research and practice will provide teachers with a menu from which to make choices and, with assistance, how to implement these into effective and realistic classroom practice.

1 The task

In a book entitled *Early literacy and the teacher*, the first questions that need to be considered are 'what is Literacy?'. This should be followed by a consideration of what the teacher is trying to achieve, in other words, 'What do we mean by development in this context?'.

WHAT IS LITERACY?

There is no widely accepted definition of the term 'literate' although it is used by many people in a number of different contexts. The ability described by the term and the degrees of proficiency implied are dependent upon the intention and experience of the speaker/writer. Whereas a report from a world missionary group might use the word literate to describe those communities which provide some sort of schooling, and an historical document could define literacy as the ability to produce a personal signature, a prospective employer might describe an applicant as literate who could display appropriate literacy skills in a letter of application, or a cabinet minister might mean someone who reads and enjoys the same works of literature as he/she does.

The *Shorter Oxford English Dictionary* (1965) defines literacy as 'quality or state of being literate' and literate as 'acquainted with letters, educated, learned'; to this could be added Chambers' definition (1980) of 'able to read or write, learned'. Alongside these there is the popular understanding of the term literacy which relates to the narrow definition of being able to read and write with perhaps rather more emphasis on the reading. The *Shorter Oxford English Dictionary* definition implies that a literate person is likely to be someone who reads a variety of 'literature' but does not necessarily write a great deal. For this reason, it is proposed to adopt as a working definition the Chambers' version which contains 'able to read and write' but also includes 'learned' which implies a further dimension from a purely mechanical skill. For being able to read and write has little purpose without the ability to *use* the skills for a variety of purposes.

Garton and Pratt (1989) in their book *Learning to be Literate* argue for the inclusion of oral language in their definition of literacy. Although it is recognised that spoken language plays a substantial part in the growth of literacy, it is not the intention here to consider spoken language as part of the *objective* of becoming literate. Rather the focus will be on reading and writing with the understanding that the ability to read and write encompasses more than responding to and producing letters on a page but includes being able and willing to use literacy when appropriate.

Also considered will be the relationship between reading and writing, at what point they are separate entities and at what point they come together to form literacy. It seems perhaps simplistic to say that writing is the composition and construction of the written form of a language, whereas reading is the interpretation of what has been written. However, there cannot be reading without writing and it is usual, though not essential, to write with the intention of it being read. Although there may be agreement about this in terms of adult literacy behaviour, this is not necessarily reflected in approaches to the teaching of reading and writing. One focus of this book will be to consider how the development of the two, side by side, facilitates the learning process for the child.

DEVELOPMENT

First let us consider what we would hope to achieve, in other words what makes a good reader and writer and what makes that person literate. Whilst education in the past has tended to assess children's literacy behaviour through narrow tests which consider one or two discrete elements of the process, and research considered here will show that many teachers, albeit unintentionally, concentrate on a narrow focus, the major aim of development literacy must be to enable children to attain their potential as learned and literate adults.

There are two major aspects of becoming a skilled reader: decoding and comprehension. Much of the debate about how the related skills should be taught centres around the relative importance of each of these aspects. Perfetti (1985) regards accurate, efficient word recognition, knowledge of orthographic structure and decoding skills as fundamental to skilled reading. However, without comprehension decoding skills are meaningless. We have all met children who go through the motions of reading the words but do not appear to have understood them.

The National Curriculum for English supports the notion of language being inseparable from its uses by stating the aim for children learning to read as 'The development of the ability to read, understand and respond to all types of writing, as well as the development of information retrieval strategies for the purposes of study' (attainment target 2). Therefore, a picture emerges of the skilled reader being one who can decode efficiently but who can also use that knowledge appropriately and effectively, continually refining his/her information processing skills. To this should be added the dimension of reading for pleasure and the acquisition of a habit for life.

There is less written about writing than about reading, but the issues revolve around the same points and it seems sensible to adopt two similar aspects to decoding and comprehension in the case of becoming a skilled writer: transcription and composition. Traditional emphasis by teachers in the initial stages has been on the correct orthographic reproduction of conventional written language forms but, whilst important, this is only one aspect of the writing process and the ability to express oneself appropriately and efficiently for both personal and practical reasons must be of even greater importance. This view is reinforced by the National Curriculum for English where seventy per cent weighting is given to attainment target 3, constructing and conveying meaning, and twenty per cent and ten per cent respectively to attainment targets 4 (spelling) and 5 (handwriting – up to level 5). Thus paramount importance is given to 'A growing ability to construct and convey meaning in written language matching style to audience and purpose' (attainment target 3).

Therefore, the good reader should not only be able to interpret the writing that he/she encounters but also use that interpretation effectively, gain pleasure from the activity when appropriate, and continue using the skills learned throughout life. In the same way, a good writer should be able to express him/herself effectively, appropriately and easily but also gain pleasure from the process when appropriate. To be literate that person should be able to use his/her knowledge and skill for a variety of purposes. Whilst a person might be judged to be literate by some definitions if he/she was an avid reader, his/her ability to generate and communicate ideas could be limited without a comparable facility in writing. Within this there are, of course, likely to be individual differences of preference.

Teaching in the early years has recently placed more emphasis on the development of literacy as a whole. Reading and writing are considered together as well as separately, placing emphasis on the reading of children's writing and the writing by children of books to be read. Indeed, both decoding and transcription, and interpretation and composition find reflections in each other. However, whilst many writers and teachers have emphasised the value of using one skill to develop another, this is not always evident in the classroom. Mortimore *et al.* (1988) did not show any correlation between successful teaching in reading and in writing in junior schools – in fact there appeared to be more correlation between successful teaching in writing and in maths. However, 'whole language' approaches to literacy teaching are still new and evidence is not yet available about the relationship between progress in reading and writing using these approaches. This book will explore ways in which the teacher can develop the two, both together and seperately, and will consider the possible benefits of these approaches.

The main intention will be to consider the role of the teacher in the pursuance of the aim of literacy. Debate is fierce about the most effective teaching methods. Research is not always helpful mainly because of the unreliability of assessment procedures. For example, research that shows children to have made great improvement on a particular measure of reading ability through certain teaching methods really only proves the effectiveness of the teaching methods to develop the abilities tested, although these may be helpful indices of wider abilities and aptitudes. There is as yet little evidence from assessments of ability on a broad front which relate to teaching method or approach. However, as data emerges from the assessment procedures of the National Curriculum, where the statements about levels of attainment cover a broad spectrum of progression, more information should be available for teachers to judge the efficacy of their strategies, although even then, the influence of socio–economic and psychological factors will need to be borne in mind.

Although debate has tended to become polarised, teaching methods can be placed along a continuum from an essentially didactic, skills-based model at one end (such as the DISTAR scheme) to a child-centred, whole-language approach where the child's interest and experience provides a starting point for learning at the other. The classroom teacher, in reality, is eclectic, choosing method and resources based on his/her particular preference and circumstances. Current practice and debate centre around the movement away from an essentially skills-based, hierarchical model towards an approach that has been variously described as 'developmentalist' (ILEA, 1988a), an 'alternative view' (Garton and Pratt, 1989), the 'minimal teaching movement' (Donaldson, 1989) etc. The intention of this book is to help practitioners make sense of this debate and to examine evidence that can assist them in adopting effective teaching approaches.

Debate revolves around three main issues:

1 Whether or not to teach skills in isolation.
2 Whether or not to use a published scheme.
3 The importance of correctness.

The teaching of skills

It is important here to realise that the debate is not primarily about whether skills are useful, but about how they are learned. The 'taught or caught' question has never been satisfactorily answered but, whether a systematic programme of teaching skills is followed or whether teachers provide an environment in which the skills can be caught, the aim is the same. Similarly, an examination of the errors children make reveals that these reflect the way they have been taught (reported by Clay, 1979). For example, an over-reliance on phonic cues to the detriment of comprehension would suggest an over-emphasis on the teaching of phonics, or a continuing inability to recognise words would suggest a lack of systematic attention to the orthography.

Traditional approaches to the teaching of reading and writing regard these as difficult activities to learn and ones which need systematic instruction before they can be used. For many years, 'reading readiness' programmes emphasised the learning of certain skills before the child was deemed ready to receive a 'reading book'. Writing was seen as a complex skill which should be taught by teachers *after* the introduction of reading because of the importance of letter sound correspondence and in which emphasis was placed on the formation of letters and on correctness. In the alternative view, the emphasis is placed on the knowledge that the child brings to the task; children are encouraged to read and write before they have the formal skills, and emphasis is placed on the purposes of literacy.

These approaches can be represented, in albeit rather simplistic form, by the diagrams below:

Traditional approach

$$\text{teaching} \quad \rightarrow \quad \text{practice} \quad \rightarrow \quad \text{use}$$

Alternative approach

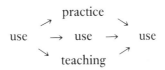

Thus it can be seen that in recent perspectives on literacy learning, the knowledge the child brings to the task is built upon by allowing him/her to use this at the same time as the teacher provides opportunities for that child to practise the skills and to be taught when appropriate.

This latter view is advocated by the Cox Report (DES, 1988b) and reflected in the National Curriculum for English which separates the composition of written language from the secretarial skills of handwriting and spelling. This does not imply that there are not skills to be taught, but that these should be taught alongside the child reading and writing and not before the child is allowed to 'have a go'.

There is some evidence (Barr, 1972; Guthrie 1973) that children learn the skills that are emphasised by the approach used, but that it is only those children of higher ability who gain further skills in spite of or in addition to what is taught. Good readers are able to build the sub skills of reading into a single process whereas those who are under-achieving gain a number of independent skills without being able to weave them into a coherent process, or become good listeners without being able substantially to take on the decoding themselves. Research into several reading programmes found that instruction did not appear to interfere with the best and average readers, but that the poorest readers tended to be doing exactly and only what they were told and appeared to have become 'instruction dependent'. It was found that the more structured the programme, the more this was the case (Clay, 1979).

On the other hand, in an analysis of the reading behaviour of eight- and nine- year-olds who had been learning to read through an apprentice-ship or shared reading approach, using miscue analysis (Goodman, 1967) and informal observation, I noticed that some children tended to over rely on the teacher when context cues failed as they had not managed to 'catch' appropriate decoding skills for themselves (Fisher, 1989). This tendency has been noted by Her Majesty's Inspectors in their survey of the reading attainment of 2,000 children (DES, 1990, para. 33).

Marilyn Jager Adams (1990) in a massive review of the current state of research into the early stages of learning to read which began as a US government-funded report on phonics, argues the importance of phonological awareness. She concludes that instruction should be designed to develop sensitivity to spellings and their relation to pronunci-ations. However, instruction often places too much emphasis on phonics in isolation. This is either, in the case of children with a great deal of literacy experience on entering school, inappropriate as it should be subordinated to the reading and writing of connected text to allow them to review and clarify what they already know, or, in the case of children with less literacy experience, not sufficiently related to reflection on the text and independent reading. Adams argues that skills should be developed 'in concert with real reading and real writing' (p. 422).

Linguists and psycholinguists who have studied the reading process and the relationship between the adult reader and the beginning reader give substance to the argument against an extensive skills-based approach. The experienced reader has been shown to process print more quickly than reading each word in sequence and, as an extension of this, reading is viewed by some as a process that cannot be learned in 'bite-sized chunks' (Goodman, 1982). However, some psychological research has emphasised the growing reliance of the developing reader on perceptual information. A major Harvard review by Chall (1983) suggested 'code emphases' had an edge on 'meaning emphases' and Mitchell (1982) criticises Goodman for placing the stress on motivation and linguistic environment without being explicit about how children should be taught. Thus Oakhill and Garnham (1988) argue that, while there are two main aspects to becoming a skilled reader (decoding and comprehension), early reading instruction should concentrate on teaching decoding without training in comprehension strategies. However, they do stress that children should learn from the outset that comprehension is the purpose of reading.

Apparent differences in findings result largely from different forms of research methodology. Psycholinguistic research tends to emphasise reading in context whereas much psychological research, whilst being more 'scientific', attempts to control variables to the extent that the effect of context is minimised. In a subject as complex as young children learning to read and write, it is difficult to tease out findings that are of use to the classroom teacher and those that may be misleading.

Despite disagreement among researchers about the relative importance at different times of the various skills and strategies, for classroom teachers there is not so much disagreement about the importance of skills but about how these are best learned. Does a programme that teaches skills in isolation or introduces skills at a time dictated by the programme rather than the informed professional in collaboration with the learner do justice to the skill of the teacher? It is, therefore, important that ways in which the teacher can plan intervention in the light of his/her knowledge of the task and of the child are considered. This is endorsed in the Cox Report (DES, 1988b) thus; 'Teachers should recognise that reading is a complex but unitary process and not a set of discrete skills which can be taught separately in turn and, ultimately, bolted together.' (para. 9, 7).

For the class teacher the decisions made will not reflect his/her view about how important it is to learn the skills of literacy so much as how he/she believes the child best learns these. Observation of young children at play, where there are opportunities for them to use both reading and writing will show that even so-called 'pre-readers and writers' are aware of some of the uses of literacy in everyday life and are quite prepared to have a go. Further analysis of their attempts will show that they have already learned some skills which should be built upon and not ignored. Giving children the opportunity to use these skills in real contexts will help with both learning and motivation and render interventions made by the teacher more appropriate.

2 Published schemes versus 'real books'

The second forum for debate revolves around the materials used. This centres more on the teaching of reading but is often reflected in the practice of learning to write; reading schemes often have associated collections of workbooks which include writing, and teachers who look for hierarchical structure outside that provided by their knowledge of the child and of literacy may incorporate these in the requirements made of the young writer. Here again it seems important to clarify the position, since there does not seem to be any disagreement as to whether young children should have available to them a range of good books of all kinds, but rather whether they should, in addition, have a reading scheme upon which to learn. It is interesting to notice how the position has changed since the First School Survey (DES, 1982a – research undertaken 1977–9) in which it was stated 'The practice of using the school library and classroom books to provide early reading material varied considerably from school to school, but in only a minority of schools were they used as an additional resource to add breadth of interest in the early stages of children's reading development' (para. 2, 12).

Now nearly all schools, according to HMI (DES, 1990) provide a wide variety of reading materials for children to enjoy, although many retain some form of sequential reading programme. Many teachers decide they need a structured approach which, they feel, can only be provided by the special materials that go with a reading scheme. In addition, the retention of a scheme can be a result of the need to demonstrate a child's progress in some way. Many teachers speak of this concern and, certainly, it takes a teacher who understands the nature of the reading process and how children may progress through this to rely on their own knowledge rather than a pre-ordained structure of a scheme. However, there are many teachers well able to do this and, with the structure supplied by the National Curriculum, there may soon be more.

Criticism of approaches which do not use a published reading scheme often implies that this results in a reduction of actual teaching with the serendipity of children's choice of book replacing structure. While it is certainly the case that an individualised approach places more emphasis on what the child *can do*, or *wishes* to read/have read to him/her, there is no reason why teachers should not introduce children to a more extensive range of strategies in reading and writing in a systematic way. However, this will be based on the judgement of the teacher about what the child already knows, not on decisions made by a distant publisher. There is as much danger in the possibility that teachers may rely on the scheme to do the teaching and the record keeping rather than applying their professional judgement and experience.

Donaldson (1989) criticises what she refers to as the 'minimal teaching movement' and implies that the use of a wide range of literature in the place of a reading scheme results in no systematic help being given to the child: 'The general conclusion has to be that the receiving of systematic help with literacy learning ... does not preclude and should not obstruct the experience of reading good books of all kinds for the joy of it' (p. 34). However, she adds to this the requirement to use a good reading or language programme which she equates with the use of simplified reading texts – it does not follow that the two should go together. Any movement that requires teachers to withhold their teaching should certainly be questioned. However, the conclusion that this is a result of a movement away from reading schemes is more difficult to justify.

Further concern centres around the language used in books. Donaldson advocates the use of a structured reading scheme that comes close to the pattern of children's speech, claiming that children first need to have acquired some basic skill at this level before being able to incorporate the features of book language into their reading. She argues that book language is too complex and varied to expect children to read from it at the start.

Children's expectations play an important part here. Where the classroom climate provides a wide range of experience of language in story reading and telling, children expect a certain type of language from books. This can be seen reflected in their writing and in their 'play reading' when they 'read' from a book, not necessarily accurately but showing an understanding of the language of books. Indeed the language of reading schemes has not always been as predictable as implied above. Much work was undertaken in the 1960s and 1970s on the patterns of children's language and that of their reading schemes (Strickland, 1962; Ruddell, 1965; Reid, 1972) which has caused improvement in the content and language of subsequent schemes. Modern schemes use language that is much more lively and engaging and closer to the children's own. Similarly, the available range of non-scheme books for children has grown enormously and the differences in linguistic structures between the two is minimal; the difference lying more in the range of language used in non-scheme books compared to similarity of linguistic structures in a reading scheme. However, since most schools now use more than one scheme (DES, 1989b) it is unclear how children benefit from reading a variety of different schemes with differing linguistic structures more than from a variety of books chosen from the full range available.

It would, of course, be unrealistic to expect children to read books of a range of types and style in the same way as they were expected to read *Janet and John*. Modern context support schemes have already moved away from the expectation that children should read every word in the early stages, and emphasis is now placed on getting at meaning. When the way the child is expected to 'read' a book is determined by the child and teacher and not by the publisher, there need be no difficulty. The demands made of the child by the teacher will depend upon that child's experience and the text chosen. Thus, the child will only be expected to read every word when it is appropriate for that child to do so.

For one child this may be after repeated readings of, for example, *The Very Hungry Caterpillar* by Eric Carle, for another the first time they pick it up from the bookshelf. These expectations are individual to the child and implemented by the teacher. Thus, another child would not be expected to read *The Very Hungry Caterpillar* accurately even after several readings, whereas he/she may be expected to read correctly his/her name on a label.

Objective, independent research evidence to show the value of using or not using a scheme is, as yet, slight and difficult to assess, since measures used are often more appropriate to a system that teaches word by word decoding. Surveys have been undertaken by local education authorities to test the efficacy of programmes in their schools (Bridge, 1989 for Leicestershire and ILEA, 1988a). These provide some interesting insights, but cannot be considered entirely unbiased or rigorous in their research methodology. They appear to show that where a new initiative has been introduced to replace reading schemes, children were judged to show more favourable attitudes to reading, and a broader understanding of the processes involved, and children who were performing below the norm at the beginning of the year did better than average. However, their approach to teaching reading was shown to cause greater levels of stress among teachers because of the degree of uncertainty of a new approach and the amount of record keeping necessary. Also pupils were slower to establish a sight vocabulary, often appearing to be at a standstill until a sudden breakthrough was followed by accelerated progress. In addition to misgivings about the reliability of the research, it must be remembered that innovation often brings initial advances because of the extra resources and enthusiasm put into the teaching programme.

Certainly under any approach children will need planned and appropriate intervention with the parts of reading they have not picked up for themselves. This has always been the case, for no reading scheme has worked for all pupils and the skilled teacher has always had to monitor progress and intervene when appropriate.

3 The importance of correctness

This leads us to the notion of the child as a risk-taker and the importance of error behaviour. Traditional expectations have been for the child to produce correct versions of his/her reading and writing from the beginning. With hindsight this seems an unrealistic request and unlike most usual forms of learning where errors are seen to be a positive part of the learning process. This practice has at times led to a certain level of tension in the teacher/child reading sessions and the production of stilted sentences from beginning writers. Whereas the eradication of error is the long-term goal of a literacy programme, it is not a necessary part of achieving that goal.

The Cox Report (DES 1988b), when referring to children learning to write, states 'Children cannot be expected to learn everything at once. A measure of tolerance of errors in different language tasks is essential' (para. 10, 8). This can also be related to the discussion in the previous section where the importance of adult expectations of children's encounters with books was stressed.

There are two issues here that will be examined in greater detail in later chapters. The first is the atmosphere of the classroom and the confidence that children have to take risks. The second is that errors are important sources of information about how children are understanding and progressing. This second issue warrants some consideration at this point because of the implicit condition that to respond effectively to errors, the teacher must have a good understanding of the processes involved and awareness of the linguistic capabilities of the children.

The centrality of linguistic awareness and a metalanguage for both teachers and children was highlighted in the Kingman Report (DES, 1988a) and followed up by Cox. The Kingman Report recommends that teacher training should involve a substantial amount of teaching of knowledge about language. Certainly an understanding of the linguistic processes of reading can help teachers to assist the child in developing strategies in this. Thus, an understanding of the difference between reading and writing will provide the teacher with an appreciation of the difficulties a beginning reader and writer may encounter. This is not to imply that interpretation of written text should be approached as something that is difficult, but that knowledge of the processes can enable the teacher to facilitate the process for the child. For example, an understanding of register will allow the teacher to talk about the appropriateness of different types of language in different situations during the reading of texts, such as, perhaps, *The Jolly Postman* by the Ahlbergs, and to model use of register in letter writing, story writing etc. which will enable children to develop this in their own explorations in writing.

Many writers from different perspectives have highlighted this need. Joyce Morris (1989) states that as early as 1958 she was convinced that teachers needed far more explicit linguistic knowledge than had been officially acknowledged up to that point. Writing from a different perspective, Margaret Meek (1982) points to the importance of teachers having the responsibility to understand the process of reading as revealed by research. Similarly Young (1988) in an article on the difference between speech and writing describes how failure to understand writing as a linguistic process prevents the teacher from fully understanding the problems that written text presents young readers.

Bereiter and Scardamalia (1985) discussed the difficulty children have in learning to compose. They considered that the difficulty is caused by the lack of interaction in writing and by the way children appear to have difficulty planning their writing on their own as they cannot think of everything they know about a topic and order it. They report that children seem to be unable to plan the structure of their composition ahead of writing it down. This results in the fact that any revision is often merely cosmetic since children have overall intentions and not sufficiently well formulated sub-goals to revise effectively. For example, knowing you want to write an exciting story is not enough; this needs to be broken down into different dimensions such as 'to create suspense'. Bereiter and Scardamalia suggest that allowing children to talk about their composition while they are doing it and the teacher assisting in the development of sub-goals and encouraging the use of procedures such as word-listing and brainstorming will help to overcome some of these problems. This work was done with older junior aged children, but it does reinforce the point that knowledge about literacy processes on the part of the teacher can assist the child in his/her development.

In a similar way linguistic awareness can inform the teacher not only of what the child is trying to do when he/she reads but also the nature of the demands made by specific programmes or methods. The statement that a particular child has not reached a certain stage may mean no more than that that child has not made sense of a particular form of instruction. For example, a child who has a below average reading age on a word recognition reading test may be able to express opinions and show understanding of texts read as a whole but find the decontextualised reading of single words very difficult.

Sensitivity to the linguistic demands of literacy will enable teachers to interpret what the child is trying to do in his/her attempt at literacy. Chapter 8 will look in some detail at three children's reading and writing with the intention of examining what this tells us about their progress. Thus it is not only the tension caused by demands of perfection that makes the expectation of correctness unhelpful but also loss of the information that less than perfect attempts can provide.

CONCLUSION

Literacy involves more than recognising and producing letters on a page. The two elements of reading and writing are linked together and a literate person needs to be willing and able to use both as appropriate. Development should be measured across the broad front, including composition and comprehension as well as decoding and transcription. As teachers we are aiming to develop all these skills and to encourage children to enjoy and feel confident in their use of literacy.

Debate rages fiercely, and has done so over many years, about the best way to teach literacy. To a certain extent the issues that make up the debate do not represent the reality of the classroom. Skills are to be learned, but the teaching of separate skills in isolation is not necessarily the best way to achieve this. Indeed there is evidence that this approach can be counterproductive. Whether one, several or no published schemes are used is of less importance than the way the teacher and children use the learning materials available to them. In all cases a wide range of experiences is important, whether supplemented by a scheme or not. Whereas the eradication of error is the long term aim of literacy teaching, errors are an important part of the learning process and can provide useful insights for teachers into how children are progressing.

Clay (1979) discusses the relationship between the teaching method and how children learn, and states that better descriptions of reading behaviour are needed both to avoid and identify early failures. She also emphasises the need for the reception class teacher to use all the various responses from her pupils as children cannot be expected to move into a narrowly conceived, pre-selected sequence of learning.

The following chapters consider what the teacher needs to know and do in order to provide an effective programme for young learners that does not rely on a publisher's external view of the situation. That is a programme which encourages the active participation of the child and which allows planned intervention on the part of the teacher in the light of his/her knowledge of the learner and of the task. The aim of the teacher at Key Stage One is to start children on the path to becoming skilled readers and writers who will continue to choose and use the skills learned into adulthood and who will be able to use their knowledge appropriately and efficiently with pleasure and ease. It is the task of the early years teacher to lay the foundations of skills and attitudes that will enable this to happen.

2 The child

The previous chapter considered what was involved in literacy learning and some of the debates that surround approaches to fostering it. This chapter takes the child as the central figure in the process and examines how children learn and what factors contribute to their learning.

The assumptions underlying the traditional views of the role of the teacher give value to that role; in which the teacher is seen to be in control of the knowledge and skills to be distributed. The idea that children come to school knowing very little and have to be taught elevates the status of the teacher. However, a shift from this to an understanding of the learning and experience that children bring to school should not detract from the importance of the teacher; rather such a shift should serve to change the nature of the role. It is the intention in this chapter to consider that research and theory can tell us about how children learn and how this can be used to inform our teaching.

The dilemma facing the teacher at Key Stage One stems, to some extent, from the opposing traditions of early years education. Bruce (1987) identifies three main stances towards the education of the young child. The 'empiricist' view takes the role of the adult as being to identify the knowledge, skills and concepts that the child lacks and to transmit these to him/her. This implies a deficit model of the child and one where children are seen as beings to be shaped in order to take their place in society. Bruce describes how this stance came to the fore in the late 1960s with the movement for compensatory education (see later in this chapter).

She places the 'nativist' stance at the opposite end of the spectrum. This stems from the thinking of Rousseau (1762). Here the child is viewed as biologically pre-programmed to develop in certain ways, helped or hindered by variations in the environment. This view results in a feeling that adults should not interfere in a child's learning and that this could be harmful. Aspects of the child's world, such as play, are seen as private and sacrosanct.

These opposing ideologies are more real in theory than in practice, but aspects of each influence thinking about children and approaches to their education. The polarisation of views that may result are unhelpful to those having to make sense of the rhetoric in the classroom. Bruce identifies a third stance: the 'interactionist' view. This provides a more sophisticated view of the child and one that provides those working in education with a model from which to work. This stance takes the role of the adult as cruicial to the development of the child, and the key to education as reciprocity. As, for example, the importance of reciprocity in conversation between adult and child is shown by Wells (1983). Adults are seen as 'the means, the mechanism by which children can develop strategies, their *own* strategies, initiatives and responses, and construct their own rules which enable their development. . . . They [children] are supported by adults who help them to make maximal use of the environment' (Bruce, 1987, p. 7).

This view of the child, together with the role of the adult in his/her education, provides a model for the teacher to work from and an important role for the teacher. The next chapter will consider in more detail how this role can unfold in the classroom. This chapter will discuss views about the child in the early years of schooling and how these may inform teachers.

The work of Piaget has been of central importance in the development of the primary school curriculum and, despite the fact that much of his work has been superseded, his influence can still be felt. The notion of children moving through stages of development that might limit their learning is no longer plausible; children have shown us what they are capable of given the right conditions. The work of McGarrigle and Donaldson, so eloquently described by Donaldson (1978), have shown us how much children can do when they understand the task. Margaret Donaldson presents a picture of children who are active and efficient learners. This view of the constructivist nature of children's learning has been reinforced in many curriculum development projects and initiatives in recent years. The most notable in language may be the apprenticeship approach to reading, in which reading is not seen to be an hierarchical system of skills to be taught in a specific order and in which the child learns to read from texts of his/her own choice alongside an adult. Also of importance is much of the work of the National Writing Project, following Clay (1975), in which the approaches developed are ones in which the child's role in the construction of language is central and in which the child's early attempts at writing are encouraged.

To this view can be added the ideas of Vygotsky and Bruner who have been of great significance in developing our understanding of how children learn. Vygotsky (1896–1934) was a Soviet psychologist and educationlist writing after the Russian revolution. His influence was suppressed in the subsequent Stalinist years and resurrected later. His work encompasses the development not only of language but also all other higher mental processes including intelligence and memory. Since the late 1970s his work has assumed importance for the study of children's developmental processes and had considerable influence on teaching and learning in the 1980s. Two of his main propositions that are relevant here are:

1   That speech in infancy is the direct antecedent of thinking at a later stage. He proposes a dual function in speech: when children speak out loud for themselves about what they are doing this is the direct precurser of thinking; and it is in conversation that children extend their control of grammatical structures and meanings.
2   More importantly his central contention is that human consciousness is fostered by the internalisation of shared social behaviour.

The implications of these propositions for teachers are great. If speech in childhood lays the foundations for a lifetime of thinking, talk in the classroom is essential. If shared social behaviour is seen as the source of learning there are further implications for the teacher's role. The idea of shared social behaviour being at the beginning stage of learning throws responsibility on those who interact with the growing child, Vygotsky (1962) proposes that what the child can do in cooperation today, he/she can do alone tomorrow. This opens up the 'zone of proximal development' which is the difference between the actual developmental level and the potential level. To assess the potential level it is necessary to present a child with a problem, the solution to which is just beyond his/her mental capacities, and allow the child to interact with another person while working out the answer. The processes by which the child works out the answer provides a better assessment of the child's intellectual capability. This 'zone of proximal development' is defined as 'the distance between the actual development level and the level of potential development as determined by independent problem solving under adult guidance or in collaboration with more capable peers' (Vygotsky, 1978, p. 84).

Jerome Bruner is one of the most notable contemporary exponents of the view that language develops in children through processes of social interaction. In Bruner's (1983) theory of the development of knowledge the human being is regarded as an active creator and learner. He regards language as a tool and considers how the child learns to use the tool effectively and efficiently. He believes that children learn language for a purpose and is concerned to explicate how the infant comes to give his/her utterances meaning and uses his/her linguistic resources to refer to things. He is primarily concerned with the communicative intent of the child and showed that the young child desires to succeed in communication.

He drew attention to the fact that young children seem able to comprehend far more complex utterances than they are able to produce. He believed that for learning to take place, appropriate social interactional frameworks must be provided – he called these 'scaffolding' (Bruner, 1977). In early language development the parent, usually the mother, provides the framework which allows the child to learn. To do this she provides contexts and routines that are familiar to the child, she remains finely tuned to the capabilities and capacities of her child and lets him/her proceed at a reasonable pace.

Both Bruner and Vygotsky were concerned with the relationship between language and thought, how children learn language and how language assists learning. Much discussion has ensued about whether assumptions can be made about how children learn to read and write from theories of how they learn to speak. Without making any such assumptions, which are open to dispute given the disparate nature of the two processes, certain conclusions can be drawn about young children's learning that have implications for the teacher:

1 The child is actively concerned with making sense of his/her world and talk underpins this active reconstruction.
2 Learning is a shared activity which should not be undertaken in isolation.
3 The child will learn more in cooperation with an adult or peer than might be thought possible from his/her Piagetian stage of development.
4 The child learns in close association with a caring adult.

INFLUENCE OF HOME BACKGROUND

Until recently, successful home learning has been associated with what was considered the 'good' home background. Although children had learned a large part of their oral language before starting school at age four or five, those children who came from homes that were judged to be linguistically or educationally unfavourable were considered to be disadvantaged from the start of their schooling. The idea that something should be done to *remediate* this is referred to as 'deficit theory', and programmes were instituted to help those children overcome their disadvantage. The work of Joan Tough (1976) in the Schools' Council Project, Communication Skills in Early Childhood, had a major influence on in-service work with teachers and emphasised the notion of appraising children's language to find out what was missing and attempting to remedy this. She takes little account of what the child's interpretation of the situation might be, nor what strengths there may be in that child's use of language which are not brought out by the context.

The advent of the use of radio microphones and video cameras has opened up the home background to more rigorous scrutiny and revealed a wealth of learning taking place in most home situations. The work of Gordon Wells (1987) in the Bristol Language Development project showed children learning language through interpersonal relationships in every home. Their findings suggest that social background is not a strong determinant of either rate or style of development, except at the extremes of the socio-economic scale. They do not argue that differences in rate of development are in no way attributable to social environment, but that there is no a priori reason to believe that such differences are based on class or code. They point to the importance of reciprocity in the conversation of adult and child in the home. In contrast to this, whilst interaction is present in the classroom, this is often asymmetrical with the teacher taking the major part, also the pedagogic intent of teachers and the greater number of children in a class can inhibit interaction.

In a similar study of thirty girls in London, Barbara Tizard and Martin Hughes (1984) followed closely the interaction between mother and child in the home and compared this to the adult-child interaction in the nursery. They studied fifteen children in each of two social class groups and found learning in the home in which the mothers discussed a wide range of topics and used recognisably educational contexts such as play, games, and stories. They isolate the special characteristics of home learning in the following ways:

1 The mothers' desire for their children to learn was often more important than the context.
2 Much general knowledge was passed over, particularly of the social world.
3 Learning occurred in a context of great meaning to the child.
4 Dialogue is as important as physical exploration.

Although this research has been criticised for the smallness of the sample, and the fact that it was all girls, the findings do seem to present a picture of children who try to extend their understandings in a persistent and local way and these findings are borne out by other research studies in addition to Wells, mentioned above. The writers suggest that the Piagetian model underestimates the child's mind and fails to appreciate the way in which adults can help children to clarify their ideas.

Juleibo (1985) in a study of a group of Canadian children showed how literacy was emerging in the home but could often disappear at school and she identified four major differences between school and home learning:

1 In the home the child usually initiated the literacy learning rather than the teacher, as happened in the school.

2 Sharing and reciprocity was usual at home, whereas at school children had to fit into a predetermined programme.

3 At home the literacy learning related to the child's previous experience and particular frame of reference, whereas in the nursery many activities were concerned only with the here and now.

4 In the home constant feedback was given to encourage a sense of success while at school errors were often corrected without explanation.

Thus it can be seen that the child brings knowledge and an ability to learn to the task of literacy learning in school. Here, however, it might be as well to introduce a note of caution from ethnographic studies such as the one undertaken by Shirley Brice Heath (1982). She studies the language and literacy events in the early lives of children from three American communities where child rearing habits vary from the white middle-class community which Heath describes as 'mainstream'. She describes the situation in the white working-class community of Roadville and the black working-class area of Trackton. The parents in Roadville buy their children books and encourage them to read but use these encounters with literacy to question and to teach skills; there is little opportunity to go beyond the immediate context or to become involved in the process of literacy. These children, when they start school, do well in the initial stages but fall behind when school requires them to move beyond the immediate and to think independently. In Trackton the ways in which children acquire language appear different, involving more imitation than interaction, there is little opportunity for literacy events and those that there are are very different in kind from the mainstream homes. However, there is a rich tradition of oral story-telling in the community and children have many language skills that are not appreciated in school. When they get to school they do not understand the kinds of questions asked in reading books, and print in isolation has little meaning for them. They consistently underachieve and by the time the school curriculum requires use of their analogical skills they have become too disenchanted with the system and have not learned the appropriate comprehension skills that they might need.

Although this research was undertaken in the United States and the community practices may be different here, there is little doubt that many schools will have children from different cultural backgrounds that may not conform to the expectations of the teacher. Whilst it is not possible for every teacher to be fully conversant with every community tradition, every teacher should be alert to the possibility of difference. The introduction of home-visiting and the greater involvement of parents in the running of schools may go some way towards heightened awareness. In addition, all teachers should provide a variety of opportunities for children to show their strengths in language; they should observe children across a range of activities and ensure that each child's capabilities are tapped as early as possible.

WHAT THE CHILD BRINGS TO THE TASK

From these findings it becomes apparent that the child comes to school already equipped with experience, knowledge and the capacity to learn. The child brings at least two important elements to the task of literacy learning in school. The first is his/her inquiring mind and innate ability to learn; he/she is already an active problem solver and this capacity should be utilised to the utmost. The second is the knowledge that he/she has already learned a great deal and with a large measure of success in his/her four or five years of life.

The notion of the child as an active problem solver who wants to find out about his/her world invites the teacher to capitalise upon this ability. Clay (1979) advocates an active and constructive approach to reading and writing, that young readers should be encouraged to depend on their problem solving abilities in their search for fluency. Although the child is certainly capable of learning skills out of context, how much more effective would that learning be if the child were to be using his/her full capacities. Thus contexts and meanings should be familiar and encourage comprehension and enjoyment.

One of the most important elements of successful learning in the home is the way in which the parent or carer knows how to place the learning within the child's own particular frame of reference, by referring to what he/she already knows and has done. Although one of the elements of school learning is the ability to take learning out of its immediate context and apply it to the wider world and to engage in 'disembedded thinking', the teacher should be aware of how the child is learning successfully at the present time and move, with the child, gradually towards more sophisticated methods.

The child has spent four or five years in a print-rich environment. We only need take a walk to the shops, turn on the television, look at what the post has brought to see letters, words and sentences all around us. Shirley Paton (1984) reports now her daughter, Cecilia, could recognise the number of her house and the letters of her name at three, and this would not be unusual. Many children can pick their favourite breakfast cereal off the shelves of the supermarket or recognise the inn sign of the Rovers' Return.

There is also evidence from studies of young readers that some children learn to read before coming to school. Although parents play an important part in this, Clark (1976) showed that the young, fluent readers in her study were able to use informed guesses to deal with new words when their parents were not around to assist them. These guesses were always related to the meaning of the text. There is also evidence that some children learn about using sound symbol correspondence (though not explicitly) before they are taught it and before they can spell correctly (Francis, 1982). Bryant *et al.* (1989) report that children who had experience and knowledge of nursery rhymes at age three showed good phonological awareness at ages five and six.

Children live in a world of story and anecdote. Some children are lucky and have stories read or told to them, but all children are familiar with the idea of story. Whether this is from eavesdropping the 'I said to him and he said to me' conversations of their parents, or whether it is from following 'Turtles' or 'Neighbours' on the television, virtually all children seem to bring to school an ability to follow simple narrative and predict outcomes – *when the situation makes sense to them*. This last point is of great importance and one that will be considered in more detail later.

THE CHILD IN SCHOOL

Whilst the child in the home can be considered to be a successful learner and an expert in this limited area, when he/she comes to school things can change. Children entering the classroom for the first time can be confused by the requirements made of them. Clay (1979) describes reading for the child entering school as a 'new and complex problem – how to act on several things he knows relating to one another to predict, and check on, the messages he finds in print' (p. 12). She tells of a child who, when talking of her attempts at reading, described her difficulty in recognising all the 'little white rivers' – she had not realised that it was the print that carried the message! However, if the task makes sense to the child, i.e. if the expectation is that the text will make sense the difficulty is at least halved. It is possible for children to have no idea of their part in the activity and to try to do what they are told with the words on the page whether or not they understand the instructions. Teachers working on the National Writing Project reported similar instances in relation to children learning to write. Children saw writing as being 'to put on the wall', 'so that you can get better at writing'. One child, when asked what was important about writing held up his index finger and said 'The finger, because if you don't put your finger on the page when you've finished a word, it won't be any good' (National Writing Project Newsletters 1 and 10).

Thus it can often appear that the child follows instructions to read or write words without grasping the purpose behind the task. The child's view of reading and also writing can be not to make sense but to *get the words right*. Thus, despite four or five years of experience of print in the environment and various language experiences in the home, it appears some children may find difficulty in relating the school task to their experience of everyday life. In this, the teacher has an important part to play by helping them to make these connections. The emphasis within the National Curriculum for English for teachers to build on the child's previous experience and to set tasks within meaningful situations is an important dimension for all teachers at Key Stage One.

This confusion about the tasks of reading and writing has been shown by several recent research studies to continue through subsequent years with teachers having difficulty in setting appropriate tasks matched to children's ability. These studies will be examined in greater detail in the following chapter but, from the point of view of a chapter on the child, they present a picture of children striving to please but not always putting their efforts into the element of the task that holds the intended learning outcome in the mind of the teacher. Bennett and Kell (1989) tell of four-year-olds who spent large amounts of time either confused or off-task while trying to gain the attention of the teacher. In a study of older infants, Bennett *et al.* (1984) write 'In their cheerfulness and industry children failed to signal to the teachers the extent of their cognitive problems' (p. 66).

However, Tizard *et al.* (1988) present one of the few recent studies of classroom activity in which the children themselves were asked for their opinion. More than half of them said they enjoyed reading and writing but they tended to over-estimate their achievement (especially the boys). Significantly, two-thirds stated that they enjoyed school although considerably fewer found it interesting.

This presents an unfortunate picture of children in school, particularly when taken with the undoubted effort that teachers put into their work. It also raises the perennial question of how far schools manage to tap the potential of all children. Whilst many children will continue to strive for success there are others who become discouraged easily and will channel their energy into other activities or withdraw. Of course, this picture does not have to be the case and the intention of this book is to consider ways in which the teacher can work with children to develop literacy in a way which makes sense to the child.

CAN ACHIEVEMENT BE PREDICTED?

Many people have tried to identify what elements at one stage act as good predictors at the next stage. Before these are considered it is worth examining the question itself. In the first place there is as yet no agreed, reliable method of measuring achievement in literacy. Tests can measure only a small part of the process and are usually on decontextualised tasks which young children, in particular, find difficult. It is to be hoped that the accumulation of data on a broad front as a result of the assessment tasks of the National Curriculum for English will provide more reliably comparable information. However, even were this the case, there is still the question as to what extent the elements considered as possible predictors of achievement are prerequisites, facilitators, consequences or only incidentally correlated.

Nevertheless, such studies abound particularly in the areas of phoneme awareness and grapho-phoneme rules. For example Tizard and Hughes (1988) report that children's knowledge of the alphabet on starting school was a good predictor of reading success at age seven. However, there is little evidence to indicate what other knowledge or experience those children may have had that could have contributed to their success. Also, following Heath's findings (1982) that children from Roadville who started well in school from a background of word and letter recognition in reading with parents, did not continue to do well when personal or individual responses were required in the later grades, we need to be hesitant in our judgements until longitudinal evidence is available that proves which knowledge or experiences are the accurate predictors.

One longitudinal study by Bradley and Bryant (1983) identified children who performed poorly on a task in which they had had to categorise words on the basis of the sounds contained in them. Two groups of these children who, it was supposed, would be expected to have difficulty learning grapheme-phoneme correspondences, were given training in sound categorisation. After two years it was found that the two training groups achieved higher reading levels than the control groups. Of the two groups, children in the one who had had their training supplemented by the use of plastic letters to illustrate how the sounds were represented by letters of the alphabet, performed better than the other training group. Even at age thirteen, Bradley (1987) found differences between the groups still existed. This implies that some form of phonic training may be helpful but that it is more effective when the children understand something of the relevance of the learning.

Other studies have shown that children who perform well on Clay's (1972) Concepts of Print test will continue to do well in reading (Lomax and McGee, 1987). This considers more than basic skills but includes knowledge about books and the way print is laid out in them.

Metalinguistic awareness is another element that causes some debate: whether the ability to reflect on language is an outcome of learning to read and write or a prerequisite for literacy. Donaldson (1978) suggests that the process of learning to read in school develops metalinguistic awareness whereas Tumner and Bowey (1984) consider this an important prerequisite. Certainly lack of knowledge of the terms used in reading and writing, such as letter, word, sentence etc., can cause confusion for the child in the classroom. Similarly the knowledge that there are different ways of saying things is something that can assist both reading and writing. Some homes will provide an environment where language is discussed whereas others will not, therefore it is important for the teacher to recognise the child's stage of progress and respond accordingly. Meta-linguistic awareness is something that has been brought to the forefront of teachers' minds by the Kingman Report and this will be discussed in greater detail in Chapter 4.

Children's error behaviour is also a good indicator, if not of potential, at least of how much sense they are making of the learning task. Both the courage to make mistakes and the ability to recognise that mistakes have been made are signs of good progress. In reading, good readers are much more likely to go back and correct an error than poor readers who appear to carry on regardless (Weber, 1970). In the same way in writing, the ability to recognise spelling errors or where the reader could become confused shows a child who has understood the concept and who is developing the skills required. The National Curriculum emphasises the importance of encouraging children to take chances in order for them to actively construct their own interpretation of the task and framework for learning.

CONCLUSION

From the sources discussed here it can be seen that children starting school are already successful and active learners who bring considerable knowledge and experience to the task of literacy learning. Children learn best when they are able to relate what they are doing to their own experience. They also learn most successfully when the learning takes place within a social context, particularly from interaction with a caring adult or more experienced child. Home is a good place to learn and, although styles may vary, there is much to be learned from the way the child has learned in the home.

The child at school, while usually eager to please the teacher, can sometimes be confused by the task set or the purpose of activities. Learning is most successful when the child understands the task and can relate it to his/her previous experience. Thus the teacher should take this into account, provide opportunities for children to interact on an equal basis with teacher and peers, and observe how the child responds to a variety of situations.

Although it is difficult to predict the potential of children, various factors have been posited as contributing to success in learning to read or write; these include knowing certain skills, having certain knowledge about the task, metalinguistic awareness and good error behaviour. However, more recently evidence from studies of children in school seems to show that the most important variable in achieving progress in reading and writing after starting school is the individual class teacher. Thus it is the teacher who will be considered in the next chapter.

3 The teacher

Whilst a good deal has been written about the process of literacy development and how the young child learns, less attention has been given to the teacher of literacy. Yet evidence is coming forward now that in fact the teacher has more effect on the child's progress after starting school than had originally been thought. It has been all too easy in the past to blame a child's lack of progress on home background or lack of innate ability. Recent studies show that, once initial differences on starting school are taken away, the overall rate of progress of a child is more affected by the class that child is in than by other factors. Mortimore *et al.* (1988), in a study of 2000 junior school children, found that it did not appear that school progress was affected by home background; in other words, that effective schools were effective for children of all backgrounds and ineffective schools were ineffective for all. Tizard *et al.* (1988), in a study of six- and seven-year-olds in London, found that school and teacher variables were more important than home variables in explaining differences in children's progress.

The debate continues as to how much direct teaching is desirable, and about which methods are the most effective to ensure lasting progress. At a time of increased teacher accountability it is interesting to look at what has been written about the role of the teacher in developing literacy and to consider evidence from studies which have examined the effect of different styles of teaching. Evidence in this area comes from a variety of sources of varying reliability. National surveys produced by HMI provide a collection of observations collated into a fairly objective report of practice. There have also been a number of research studies undertaken. These set out to collect data using a variety of selection and assessment procedures which attempt to achieve objectivity but may be limited by the parameters of the study. In addition there are the small-scale research reports produced by local education authorities which examine the efficacy of the teaching in their schools. While providing some useful indications these may be value-laden and unrepresentative.

All studies that judge the effectiveness of teaching can only be as reliable as the measures used to assess children's performance as a result of that teaching, although they may indicate aptitude in a wider range of skills and activities. For example, procedures that assess children according to word recognition can only be a measure of success at teaching or learning to recognise words. This would tell us little of the efficacy of the programme on a broader front such as National Curriculum procedures intend to address. Alternatively, assessment of wider issues is difficult to undertake and limited by the subjective nature of the observations. Thus, it can be seen that findings need to be read critically for whatever indications they can give us, without unquestioning belief in their reliability.

In this chapter the different types of study described above will be reviewed. This will be followed by a discussion of the ambivalence felt about the role of the teacher in recent years, particularly following the Plowden Report (1967). Next an attempt will be made to draw out from the reported research studies and elements discussed in the earlier chapters what the role of the teacher should be in developing literacy in the classroom.

HMI REPORTS

It is a well known fact that the number of publications from the Department of Education and Science have proliferated in the last ten to fifteen years. Several of these have considered the teacher's role. The HMI Survey *Primary Education in England* (DES, 1978) looked at teachers in classes of seven-, nine- and eleven-year-olds. They found that less than one in twenty teachers relied mainly on an 'exploratory method' of teaching while about three-quarters employed a mainly didactic approach and that where they used a combination of approaches children scored better on the NFER reading and maths tests. In the vast majority of classes, reading schemes and courses were used to provide material at the right level of difficulty and were used regularly. HMI affirm unequivocally 'On the evidence of this survey teachers . . . work hard to ensure that children master the basic techniques of reading and writing. There is little support for any view which considers that these aspects of language are neglected in primary schools' (Para. 5, 46). At this time HMI report that the use of graded reading schemes in classes of seven-year-olds was universal but they felt that children received little encouragement to extend their reading repertoires. Children were quite often asked to comment on what they had read but rarely to discuss it. The inspectors found a limited range of types of writing; personal writing increased with the age of the pupils but they report little evidence of older children being presented with writing tasks that required them to present a coherent argument and little opportunity for self-initiated writing. They, like the Bullock Report (DES, 1975) also complain of extensive copying from reference books.

Four years later the First School Survey (DES, 1982a) was published, although this referred to circumstances found in schools in 1977–9. It also found great emphasis placed on the teaching of reading with a combination of the 'look and say' and 'phonic' methods being employed. Many schools were criticised for an 'unduly long concentration on the basic reading scheme, and few instances were seen of children becoming engrossed in books. Although there were book corners or libraries in most schools, in only a few were these used to add breadth and interest to the early stages of children's reading. It was also felt that children were introduced too soon to a reading scheme and phonic practice with the result that some were confused and made little progress. There was found to be a fair variety of types of writing undertaken in most schools but some schools were criticised for 'unproductive time being spent on English exercises, of a stifling of individuality by stereotyped tasks or copying, and of low levels of aspiration' (2.24). They recommended that all children should have frequent opportunities for writing of a descriptive and expressive nature.

A report on practice of probationary teachers was published in 1982 (DES, 1982b). Amongst other issues this considered the teacher's language work. HMI comment that, while some teachers interact well with their pupils, others used a high proportion of 'closed' activities where children had little opportunity to question. A number of factors were identified as being most frequently associated with what HMI define as 'good practice'. These include: pupils' participation, interest and involvement; good organisation showing balance, variety and effective use of resources; lively discussion using appropriate questioning techniques; good relationships with mutual respect; good planning, preparation and match.

The findings of the survey of reading teaching in schools undertaken in 1989 (DES, 1989b) reiterate some previous points and introduce some new ones. They report that most schools use one or more graded reading schemes supported by other books. Some had adopted what HMI describe as 'an apprenticeship approach' but this was usually supported by some form of commercially produced scheme which was used with some children. Record keeping in years one and two came under particular criticism for recording only *what* was read not *how* it was read. Good practice observed included records of attitudes and skills and a reading interview based on a core text.

In general, it was found that good readers were underchallenged and teaching showed insufficient differentiation. In schools where books were valued, silent reading sessions were usually successful. However, poor use was made of reference books. There was often lack of variety and experiment in response to texts, no clear objectives linking policy to classroom practice and too little feedback. It is also recommended that schools develop their assessment procedures to provide a broader range of strategies and a more varied reading diet in response to assessment.

A survey published a year later (DES, 1990) again emphasises the high priority given to teaching children to read at Key Stage One. They again report that the great majority of teachers (almost eighty-five per cent) use a blend of methods to teach initial reading. Record keeping in this report was found to be adequate or better in about two-thirds of the schools, particularly at Key Stage One. The report criticises teachers who adopt a narrow approach either using, as described by the teachers themselves 'real books' (five per cent), or 'phonic teaching' (about three per cent); both approaches were found to have limitations. Children in the classes that had too narrow a focus on phonics were found to have too few strategies to tackle new words and did not read for meaning even when they read the words accurately. Teachers who described their approach as using 'real books' are reported to assume that children would gain independence with minimal help from the teacher. Children were seen to have a growing interest in books but their accuracy was limited and they had too few skills for decoding print. This is not to say that HMI do not agree with the use of phonics or of real books, rather that a narrow approach limits the children's progress. Those schools that were judged to achieve high standards of reading shared four common characteristics:

- a firm leadership that established reading as a high priority in the school;
- a clear, well-documented, balanced reading policy;
- a well-managed classroom practice with work matched to individual needs; and
- a wide variety of appropriate books and other materials, effectively organised.

STUDIES OF CLASSROOM PRACTICE

In addition to the HMI surveys there have been some research studies undertaken which have provided useful insights into what the teacher does in the classroom and, in some instances, how effective this is. The majority of these have been in junior classrooms but more recently there has been a growing awareness of the importance of infant education. The picture emerges of extremely hardworking and conscientious teachers doing their utmost to enable children to learn the skills of language (and other curriculum areas) but sometimes demonstrating an ineffectiveness of classroom management that renders some, but by no means all, of their efforts in vain. In addition to this, there is indication of a conflict in teachers' minds about the nature of their role. This is evidenced in the studies by the sometimes contradictory messages teachers can give to children about their intentions.

Junior classrooms

An early study by Bennett (1976) in which traditional teaching methods were reported to be more effective than progressive ones in the seven to eleven age range, and which had a major impact on the popular view of teaching, was based on the teachers' own judgement of their teaching style, and the conclusions drawn have since been shown to be flawed in assessment techniques, although re-analysis resulted in similar, though less extreme differences. As a result, the suspicion attached to 'progressive' teaching methods has remained, although there is no clear definition or agreement on what either opponents or proponents might label as 'progressive'.

Galton and Simon (1980), in the ORACLE study, conducted research in classrooms and the team made their own assessments of teaching styles from cluster analysis and observational data based on three years' work. They examined the different organisational strategies employed by teachers in junior classes. They found a high priority afforded to language but comment that, as reading at least is individualised, the individual pupil spends less time on language or reading than would appear from a study of the time spent by the teacher. They go on to report that the emphasis given to basic skills as a proportion of the total observed lesson time did not correlate positively with progress.

They summarise by concluding that, when the effects of gender, pupil type and teaching styles are considered together, only teaching style appeared to have an independent effect on progress. This was found to be the case even with pupil types where there are differences in the amount of time spent working. In successful teaching styles motivation was not found to affect progress, but in less successful styles well-motivated pupils were found to make better progress. They identify some common characteristics among the 'top three' styles:

- There were above average levels of interaction with the pupils, that is:
  higher than average proportion of routine and open-ended questions;
  more factual statements;
  more feedback given; and
  less statements about task supervision.
- Teachers devoted considerable effort to ensuring that routine activities proceeded smoothly.
- Children were encouraged to work by themselves towards solutions to problems – i.e. teachers either gave such clear instructions that they did not need repeating or they expected children to work out for themselves what they should be doing.

The Schools Council Project *Extending Beginning Reading* (Southgate *et al.*, 1981), undertaken in the mid-1970s and published in 1981, considered reading in National Curriculum years three and four (seven to nine years). They again found teachers giving reading a high priority but expending an enormous amount of effort in trying to hear children read, often at the same time as doing many other things. Paradoxically it was found that where teachers placed less emphasis on hearing children read, these children made more progress in reading. In these classes more time was given to uninterrupted silent reading and talking to children about the books they had read. The recommendations that resulted suggested that children should have more choice of the books to read, that time spent reading to the teacher should be quality time spent in discussion and appraisal, and that teachers should consider ways of avoiding the lengthy queues that tended to develop.

In a search for what makes schools 'effective', Mortimore *et al.* (1988) followed 2000 junior school pupils through four years of classroom life in fifty schools in ILEA. They found that 'the school makes a far greater contribution to the explanation of progress than is made by pupils' background characteristics and age' (p. 204). Like the Galton and Simon study (1980), they stress that observation reveals that teachers do not always teach in the way they describe to researchers, for example in the amount of class teaching undertaken.

In their consideration of the language curriculum they found that almost all teachers in the sample (ninety-five per cent) taught at least some language as a distinct subject and nearly half included it in project work. Content covered included creative writing, story telling, poetry, comprehension, spelling, grammar and oral work. Most teachers did not rely on a particular text book and a few used none at all. However, the vast majority of teachers made use of reading schemes although the use declined over the years. In the first year (National Curriculum Year 3) all teachers used at least one scheme, and most made use of more than one. The amount of time teachers spent on hearing reading fell from just over five per cent in the first year to almost two-and-a-half per cent in year three (National Curriculum Year 5). There is no mention of the quiet reading time when all children and the teacher read, advocated by Southgate et al. (1981), but they do report that ten per cent of the time spent hearing an individual child read was spent in talking to the child and no mention is made of teachers trying to deal with other matters at the same time. Three per cent of teacher time was spent reading stories although, surprisingly, this was less in year one than in year three. In eighty per cent of the classes children were given different work according to ability but not according to age.

They found reading ability at one age to be a good predictor of reading at a later age but that progress in maths and writing was subject to greater flexibility. However, once initial starting points had been taken into account they found the school attended to be responsible for twenty-four per cent of the variation in pupils' reading progress between years one and three, although in writing, the school accounted for only thirteen per cent of the variation. Those schools that had a good effect on reading progress did not necessarily do so with writing; in fact there was more correlation between attainment in maths and writing.

As a result of their study the authors identified some key factors for effective schools which involved a happy, supportive and supporting staff and a structured framework which allowed some freedom for individual teachers. Within classrooms several factors were found to be important, these included:

- flexible organisation to maximise individual contact with pupils;
- a limited focus within sessions;
- effective means of record keeping;
- work forecasts;
- school-wide policies and consistent use;

- parental involvement where this was more than a PTA; and
- discussing and explaining the purpose of work.

There were also factors that had a negative effect on performance. For example, where the headteacher placed a narrow emphasis on basic skills the effect was negative on both basic skills and non-cognitive areas.

In an early study about one aspect of the writing process, Peters (1970) found that the behaviour of teachers was the most important factor in children's individual progress in spelling. Although socio-economic factors might determine the starting point, she found that the teacher's role in the teaching of spelling was crucial. She identified five strategies that were found in successful teachers of spelling in the junior school:

- that the teachers were constant in attitude to spelling;
- that words given on word-lists were related to children's usage and not taken from published word-lists;
- that teachers spent time teaching spelling as well as giving lists to be learned;
- that teachers ensured that spellings were not corrected by 'rote' (i.e. writing out the word three times), but that the method employed should be 'rational' where teachers had worked out a way for children to correct their mistakes autonomously; and
- that children should be encouraged to try out words for themselves before asking or looking them up.

Peters emphasised the importance of learning letter formation and letter sequences at the junior stage to assist the learning of spelling. She also found that the child's self-image of him/herself as a speller was very important.

Infant classrooms

While the studies reported so far have concentrated on junior classrooms, the *Quality of Pupil Learning Experience* (Bennett, *et al.*, 1984) turned attention to the whole task process in the top infant classroom (National Curriculum Year 2). They found tasks demanding practice of existing knowledge, concepts or skills predominated particularly in language work and that teachers failed to implement intended demands either through poor or misdiagnosis or through failures in task design. High attainers received less new knowledge and more practice than low attainers and, while teachers saw tasks that were too difficult, they rarely found tasks that were too easy.

They found little evidence of an integrated language curriculum in operation and the majority of language tasks was aimed at the development of writing skills. Seventy per cent of these writing tasks were specifically to practise writing and emphasis was on the surface features. Teachers were often found to stress procedural rather than cognitive aims to the children with the result that children may have misunderstood the language demands of the school. For example, teachers sometimes emphasised the careful colouring of a phonic worksheet rather than the sound that it was intended to teach. In a similar way teachers sometimes tended to concentrate their comments to children on a limited range of criteria, particularly neatness, punctuation, spacing and quantity, regardless of their stated aims or of the instructions they had given to the children. It is hardly surprising that children themselves emphasise these elements as being important factors in good writing. There are other cautions to be drawn from this study. In two of the classes teachers did a lot of work on punctuation but, according to the monitoring system used in the research, these children did not improve and in fact one class deteriorated. In contrast, the class shown to be the most inventive in their writing did not spend an inordinate amount of time on imaginative writing but covered a range of types of writing including free choice, topic writing and poetry.

Reading was observed to comprise phonic tasks, comprehension tasks and reading to the teacher and, like Southgate *et al.* (1981), Bennett *et al.* criticise the practice of hearing children read while attending to other matters. They found that the majority of interaction in classrooms was about spelling. Despite the criticism of the management of the teachers observed in the study, it is recorded that significant progress was observed in the quantity of writing produced by the children and in the quality of the organisation of passages. However, they found large differences between classes in terms of what was attempted and what was obtained. This was not found to be attributable to socio-economic factors in the catchment area but arose rather from decisions made by individual class teachers or from the design of school schemes.

The conclusions drawn by the authors of this study relate more to the teacher as a manager of time and of learning than to any implication that teachers are not able or conscientious in their work. They criticise the air of 'crisis management' found in some classrooms and the teachers' apparent inability to diagnose needs appropriately. There are several indications of ways in which the teacher can render his/her work more effective and these will be considered in more detail in the second part of this book.

The findings of Tizard and Hughes (1984) have been discussed in the previous chapter in relation to the way young children learn in the home. However, these authors make some interesting comments about the role of the teacher in the nursery school. This has traditionally been different from that of the infant school teacher and Tizard and Hughes found it involved suggesting and stimulating play, demonstrating craft or new play activities and talking to children about what they are doing. There was found to be no explicit teaching of reading or writing but the foundations were laid for these skills through activities such as pattern recognition, hand-eye co-ordination exercises, developing children's spoken language and their understanding of the relationship between stories and the printed text. They found little direct teaching and less adult child interaction than in the home and what there was tended to be briefer and more adult-dominated. They comment 'in the case of the staff, their educational aims tended to be pursued quite independently of the children, and often without any relation to their interests' (p. 212). They advocate more opportunity for adult/child interaction of the kind found in the home and higher expectations of the children.

Similar findings to Bennett et al.'s earlier study (1984) are reported in a more recent study by Bennett and Kell (1989) in which they consider the lot of the four-year-old in school. Unlike the findings of primary school survey in relation to primary school children in general, Bennett and Kell found that few of the teachers who had four-year-olds in their classes were trained for or experienced with this age group. They reveal that while affective aims were stressed in the philosophy expressed by the teachers, cognitive aims dominated in the curriculum. Task appropriateness of children's classroom activities were examined in terms of teacher intentions, presentation, match, task implementation and assessment. They found the highest priority given to spoken language and early number with play having very low priority, and children were often found to be confused and off-task, waiting to gain the attention of the teacher who had made his/her initial intention unclear. One task in four was judged to be mismatched with slightly more overestimates than underestimates and even where match was appropriate there was sometimes failure of implementation due to shortcomings in classroom and task management. This was accompanied by ineffectual task assessment and diagnosis which caused inappropriate follow-up intentions: success appeared to be related not to teacher intentions but to affective characteristics 'busy work was often equated with appropriate or successful work' (p. 74).

In order to improve teaching and learning Bennett and Kell recommend changes in the way reception teachers organise their teaching to become better managers of learning. Like Mortimore *et al.* (1988) who found that to discuss and explain the *purpose* of work was an element of successful classrooms, Bennett and Kell suggest the use of 'advance organisers' in order to improve children's understanding of the tasks required of them. They recommend that teachers structure the information that children are to encounter in order to provide an intellectual scaffold. They found that teachers knew what their intentions were and planned accordingly but did not pass these intentions on to the children, often emphasising a different element such as the neat colouring in of a phonics worksheet. They suggest teachers overcome the problem of match, monitoring and diagnosis by less individualisation and that they consider children as 'social beings' rather than 'lone scientists' (Bruner and Harste, 1987) and that learning should be seen as a cooperative endeavour.

Tizard *et al.* (1988) studied the effects of school and parents on infant progress with particular attention to ethnic group, social class and gender factors. This was a longitudinal study and interesting in that it compared children from the same school and area but different racial origins, and in this way lessened the variables affecting results. They describe the language curriculum as demonstrated by the middle infant classes. In reading, six per cent used one published reading scheme, eighty-eight per cent used a variety of schemes, fifty-nine per cent used *Breakthrough to Literacy*, and almost all teachers supplemented the schemes to some extent. For writing, teachers used *Breakthrough to Literacy*, language workbooks, tracing and copying, and some form of stimuli or 'news' as a starting point for writing. In maths there was greater reliance on published materials but the authors comment that the teachers' use of published schemes was eclectic and flexible in both maths and reading. In language, teachers moved from early emphasis on the mechanics, through rules for deciphering and reproducing text and on to reading for meaning and the production of longer written texts. In handwriting they moved from tracing to copying to producing own text; it seems that at the time of the project (1982–5) the significance of emergent writing was almost unknown. (i.e. children's early attempts at writing which, while not necessarily being conventionally correct or even legible to anyone other than the writer, make sense to the child and demonstrate the knowledge about writing that he/she already has).

There is support for the implications of earlier studies in that they too show indications that children do better at some schools and with some teachers than others. Although the sample was not large, results do suggest that teachers make more difference than the school and, particularly, progress made in reading in the reception class varied enormously. Although Tizard *et al*'s sample was not large, their findings point in similar directions to the previous studies in that they emphasise the importance of a coherent policy for reading, the effect of teacher expectations on the curriculum covered, the value of effective assessment and the importance of the management of learning for effective progress.

LOCAL EDUCATION AUTHORITY STUDIES

A recent smaller study undertaken in Hackney (ILEA, 1989a) attempted to compare the reading programmes used in their schools and to evaluate the success of an in-service course. This study reinforced the idea of the teacher as being the most important factor in effecting progress in literacy. Although the study set out to discover whether teachers described as 'developmentalists' were more effective than 'traditionalists', they found that emphasis on literacy and a coherent school policy within a supportive framework was actually more important than the type of programme adopted. Within the classroom they found five broad areas that were identified as relating to progress:

1 Prominence of literacy in the curriculum, 'In general, pupils who made the most progress in reading were those who were stimulated by a variety of approaches to literacy and where literacy occupied a prominent place in the curriculum' (p. 10). This was evidenced by hearing children read two or three times a week, using a wide range of resources and specific reference to spelling rules (but not spelling tests).

2 A pupil-centred approach, where the teacher paid particular attention to the interests of the pupils, allowing them to choose books to read and to have read and discussing these. Also allowing pupils to choose what to write about particularly their own projects and interests.

3 A supportive framework. The building of confidence in writing was found to be related to progress in reading. Children were grouped for writing, given feedback according to their individual efforts, had their work marked, discussed with them and displayed or presented in some way. 'Overall, it would seem that children made greater progress if they worked within a supportive framework receiving constructive, personalised feedback from the teacher' (p. 11).

4 Record keeping. Highly specific records were shown to be more

effective than records such as colour-coding or recording stages of the reading scheme. Records based on miscue analysis were judged to be the most effective.

5 Parental involvement in the learning process as part of home–school liaison schemes, particularly when organised by the class teacher or a group of teachers.

AND ELSEWHERE . . .

The studies reported so far have been undertaken in the United Kingdom. There is also evidence from the United States about the effectiveness of teacher styles, but findings must be considered cautiously as curriculum design in the US is so different from that of the UK and starting ages of pupils differ. However, evidence from these studies also demonstrates the importance afforded by teachers to the teaching of literacy and there is further evidence to support the central role of the teacher in the structuring of the young child's literacy development (Van Dongen, 1979; Deffenbaugh, 1976; Minns, 1988 and Durkin 1988). Evidence from these studies shows the importance of teacher expectations (Rist, 1970 and Michaels 1980), the value of building upon the child's previous experience and creating a real literacy environment (Beardsley and Marecek-Zeman, 1987; McGee, 1986 and Hoffman and Kripping 1988), the relationship between early writing and reading (Tway, 1983) and particularly the way in which early writing can assist reading development instead of the reverse as was previously supposed (in collected papers Utah, 1978). Also stressed is the importance of the teacher as a manager of learning, particularly with reference to the tendency to orient towards other children while hearing individuals read (Eder, 1982) and the value of teacher pupil interaction (Woodward, 1988).

SUMMARY

A summary of these findings from the English studies discussed can be seen on Table 1. From these studies it becomes evident that the effectiveness of the individual teacher is a crucial element in the progress made by the child. Perhaps more important than the programme or method used is the relationship between the child and teacher and the confidence of the teacher in the methods employed.

Table 1 *A summary of the findings into English primary classrooms 1980–1989*

Recommended teacher behaviour	T1	B1	B2	T2	H	M	O	HM
High level of interaction including opportunities for extended conversation and higher order questioning.	+	+				+[a]	+	+
Good match showing high expectations of ability and interest.	+	+		+				+
Good task design and evaluation including consideration of cognitive outcomes.		+	+					
Good assessment and record keeping.		+	+	+[b]	+			+
Opportunities for cooperative learning.			+	+	+	+[c]		
Feedback to the children with praise and positive attitude.					+	+	+	+
Whole school policy.				+	+	+		
Parental involvement.				+	+[d]	+		
Management skills such as advance organisers, routine.		+	+			+	+	
Encouraging active involvement, allowing freedom to make errors and find solutions within a framework.	+	+				+	+	
Relevance and purpose to the task, discussed with and understood by children.			+	+	+			
Limited focus within sessions.						+		
Range of activities and approaches within literacy tasks.		+		+				+

Key

T1	Tizard and Hughes (1984)
B1	Bennett *et al.* (1984)
B2	Bennett and Kell (1989)
T2	Tizard *et al.* (1988)
H	Hackney (ILEA, 1988)
M	Mortimore *et al.* (1988a)
O	Oracle (Galton and Simon, 1980)
HM	HMI surveys in 1980s

Notes

[a] This mainly refers to interaction with class or groups; too much interaction with individuals was found to be counter-productive.
[b] Particularly highly specific or diagnostic records, not just books read.
[c] Too much of this proved to have negative results.
[d] When this was more widely based than a PTA (Mortimore), and when arranged by the class teacher (Hackney), Tizard found parental involvement in reading did not aid learning.

However, certain indications can be drawn from the studies and a picture of an effective literacy teacher for young children emerges. This is of someone who gives a high priority to literacy and provides a wide variety of literacy experiences for the children. This does not necessarily imply a heavy emphasis on the teaching of certain skills but emphasis on the experiences and resources provided for the children. It should be a person who is an effective manager of learning and who designs and matches task to pupil appropriately. The effective teacher will be someone who provides opportunities for interaction about literacy events within the classroom between the child and adults and between the child and his/her peers. A teacher who can successfully and effectively monitor the child's progress, plan a suitable programme for that child and provide feedback to him/her about that progress all within a supportive environment.

TEACHER ROLE

The role of the teacher in learning has been a subject of discussion for many years. The Plowden Report (1967) was criticised for ignoring the positive role of the teacher for fear of authoritarianism (Peters, 1969). It has been suggested that the picture of good practice presented by Plowden was idealised; although much was written about learning, there was little written about teaching. Only one method of teaching was presented: the ideal of total individualisation of learning. This has been taken up in many primary schools but the large number of children in classes and the limited resources available make this an ideal that is difficult to realise.

Hall (1987) in an article in the *Times Educational Supplement* criticises the Plowden Report for giving 'the green light to the introduction of many unproven progressive ideas in our primary schools' (p. 24). She centres her criticism on the integrated day which she implies signifies the absence of sustained input by the teacher causing children to pursue interests at a superficial level only. She discusses the way choice can cause a child to waste time or fritter it away without the teacher monitoring what is happening. The integrated day is an organisation system which can either work in the way described by Hall, or which can actually enable the teacher to spend time teaching targetted groups rather than the whole class. Choice can also be used in a number of ways which do not have to be as she describes. However, she pinpoints an important issue: the fact that the rhetoric of the Plowden Report, which emphasised learning over and above teaching, denied teachers a positive role. This, Hall states, has caused teachers to 'succumb to a massive loss of nerve and themselves equate class teaching in all its variety with a rigid formalism which had long since disappeared'.

Certainly the ideologies of infant education which were endorsed by Plowden: knowledge of development, individual differences, that children should be 'agents of their own learning', and the value of play in learning, sit uneasily with a prescribed National Curriculum and national assessment procedures. However, they do not need to be mutually exclusive.

Alexander (1988) examined teachers' views on the divide between the Plowden ideal and the demands on a teacher in the 1980s. He found some teachers experienced a great sense of mismatch between the ideal and reality, they felt themselves to be walking an 'ideological tightrope'. Some teachers dealt with this by having half the curriculum flexible and the other half (usually maths and language) non-negotiable. Teachers described feelings of guilt associated with structure, but guilt also in relation to the need for accountability and control. Alexander argues that these feelings are avoidable; flexibility is more about the freedom to think and act independently than having to conform to a perceived approved style.

The rationalisation of the ideologies as provided by Bruce (1987), referred to earlier in Chapter 2, demonstrates how education is moving away from the polarisation of the conflicting ideologies of empiricism and nativism which was, anyway, more real in theory than in practice. However, when approaches are over-simplified and set in unrealistic opposition to each other, as in the tabloid view of education, little help is given to the confidence of teachers who try to make sense of the conflicting messages received.

It is the intention of this book to discuss practice within a philosophy that acknowledges the importance of the child as an agent of his/her own learning and the central tenet of language learning as making meaning, but that also acknowledges the reality of classroom situations and the desire of all teachers to provide an effective learning programme for all children. This cannot and should not deny the value of structure and control but recognises that good structure and control will allow children the freedom to learn.

In relation to literacy learning in particular, how can teachers keep some notion of child-centredness while maximising their time and ability to allow children to achieve their potential? Since results from studies described earlier indicate more than direct teaching from a published programme, what roles should teachers adopt? This is not to ignore the role of the teacher as 'instructor', as this is certainly one part of the teacher's role, but for the purposes of this book it will be refined into the other roles discussed. Each chapter will consider to what extent the teacher should intervene as a facilitator and to what extent intervention should involve direct teaching.

Gray (1980) in a review of Galton and Simon wrote 'the ways of failing as a teacher may be limited but there may be several alternative paths to excellence'. Indeed, various authors and groups have identified the main components of the teacher's role; their choice reflecting their own particular concern and emphasis. Cazden (1983) proposed three models in which the adult provides assistance to the child learning language: scaffolding, models, and direct instruction; whereas Smith (1988) summarises the basic role of the teacher as encouraging learners to 'join the literacy club', i.e. to demonstrate to children the enjoyment and relevance of reading and writing.

It is above all, with the approaches to literacy learning that do away with the traditional trappings of a reading scheme together with copy writing and spelling books, that teachers feel under most pressure. It is these approaches that are referred to by their critics as involving 'minimalist teaching' (Donaldson, 1989). Yet this is far from the case; there have always been a few teachers who do as little as possible, but these could just as easily be those who use a reading scheme as any other method. Indeed it can be argued that a reading programme that provides workbooks and reading books to follow one after the other could lull the teacher into a false sense of security.

Various groups have tried to identify the role of the teacher in early literacy development. Smith (1988) identifies two functions for the teacher in guiding children towards literacy: demonstration of uses for writing and helping children to use writing themselves. Two further examples of roles would be:

1 The Leicestershire support service's booklet on learning to read through the 'story method' describes three roles for the teacher of reading:
   (a) to lead each child to want to read;
   (b) to act as his model; and
   (c) to provide the time and books to share.

2 The Manchester Writing Project, as Czierniewska (1988) describes, categorised the teacher's roles in the teaching of writing as:
   (a) facilitator – well-resourced and enabling experimentation and collaboration;

(b) model of all literacy behaviours;
(c) adviser who intervenes at key points to support and extend the process; and
(d) observer who watches, monitors progress and gives a sense of achievement.

The Non-statutory Guidance for English at Key Stage One (DES, 1989b) suggests various roles for the teacher of reading and writing. For reading, it suggests the teacher should be:

'a responsive and interested listener to children's reading of their own writing and chosen texts;
an organiser of opportunities to read with other adults and children;
a partner/guide in discussion of reading experience;
a reader of books and children's own stories, in order to provide an example and encourage interest;
a support, helping children to use all the available cues to making sense of their reading;
a monitor of reading development;
a recorder of progress.'

For writing it suggests the teacher should be:

'an organiser of adults other than teachers who can work alongside children, 'scribing' for them, or using a keyboard, and enabling them to compose at greater length than they could on their own (POS 18);
an editorial consultant;
a praiser of achievement;
an example of adult writing behaviour;
a setter of procedures;
a setter of standards;
a recorder of progress;
a monitor of learning development.'

In later chapters various roles for the teacher of young children that have emerged from the preceding discussion will be described and discussed with particular relevance to literacy and the National Curriculum. These will fall under the headings of: facilitator; model; manager of learning; and assessor. 'Facilitator' because it is the teacher who has to make decisions, within the National Curriculum and school policy. These decisions will be about the classroom environment, the learning context, resources used, access to these resources and about the ethos of the classroom. 'Model' because by modelling appropriate literacy behaviour the teacher can demonstrate many of the important skills that children are learning. Seeing these used in context can give meaning to lessons learned. 'Manager of learning' because so much of the research reported earlier has demonstrated that it is inefficient management by teachers that causes less effective teaching programmes and can also cause teacher stress. A good manager can organise his/her teaching to enable children to gain most from the classroom environment and give the teacher time to focus his/her work with groups or individuals. 'Assessor' because without the monitoring of development the teacher would be unable to evaluate the effectiveness of his/her teaching or formulate further plans.

Each role will be examined in terms of what the role could involve and why it is considered to be important.

CONCLUSION

Primary teachers have suffered in recent years from a sense of uncertainty about their role. The ideologies of child centredness and individualisation have placed impossible pressures on teachers of large classes with often inadequate resources. The criticisms ever present in the press only add to their concern. However, several studies in the 1980s of the factors that go to make a good teacher show the efforts made by teachers to achieve a high standard and the high profile awarded to literacy in the infant classroom. They also show how important an element the individual teacher is in the progress made by the child.

It is possible to draw certain conclusions about the role of the teacher from the studies considered. The effective teacher of literacy should give a high priority to reading and writing and provide a wide range of experiences for children to both use literacy and to see it used. The teacher should also be an effective manager of the classroom situation, providing opportunities for interaction and appropriately designed and matched tasks for the children. He/she should also be able to monitor progress effectively in order to plan a suitable programme and give feedback to the learner.

This indicates the roles of facilitator, model, manager and assessor which will be discussed in the subsequent chapters. First, however, it is relevant to examine the National Curriculum for English at Key Stage One in order to consider what legal requirements there now are for the teacher of literacy and to what extent these reflect work as discussed in the preceding chapters.

4 The National Curriculum

In the first three chapters of this book the main components of literacy learning in schools were discussed. Added to these, now, must be the National Curriculum which makes law certain statements about the kind of provision that should be found in classrooms and the levels of attainment that children might be expected to have reached.

It is clear that the National Curriculum does not entirely clarify the role of the teacher. Although it is intended to prescribe content rather than teaching methods, some aspects of teaching are implied. For example, the need for teachers to allow children to experiment with their spellings as in Attainment Target 4, Level 2, 'produce recognisable (though not necessarily correct) spelling of a range of common words', and 'recognise that spellings have patterns and begin to apply their knowledge of those patterns in their attempts to spell a wider range of words'. The requirement that each child is assessed individually for aspects of the core curriculum requires a large amount of individualisation in learning to cater for the different levels within the class. Therefore, it can be seen that dilemmas will continue to be presented to teachers which only their own experience and philosophy can answer.

Much has been written about the reasons for and the development of the National Curriculum, but it is only relevant here to examine these in relation to literacy learning. In recent years there has been considerable public outcry to 'improve standards', yet consideration of reasons for this are not founded on statistical evidence. The Assessment of Performance Unit (APU) who tested standards regularly at national level from 1978–1988 show that, in fact, standards of literacy were rising at age eleven in that period (APU 1988, 1991). However, there is justifiable disquiet about the extent to which young people are able to cope with the increasing literacy demands of work and leisure. Also there is the concern that, while children may leave school with the ability to read and write sufficiently well to get through the necessary examinations, many do not continue to read or write for pleasure after this.

Despite the lack of substance to the charge that standards are falling, concern felt by government and public in general is reflected in the fact that there have been three major enquiries into the teaching of English in fourteen years chaired by Bullock (DES, 1975), Kingman (DES, 1988a), and Cox (DES 1988b). The Bullock Report emphasised the role of language in personal development, stressed the importance of a broad language curriculum with the four aspects of language – reading, writing, speaking and listening – treated as a unity. It also advocated that all schools should have a member of staff with specific responsibility for language and a policy statement about language teaching in the school. Whilst this latter recommendation has certainly taken effect and there was some considerable effort put into post-Bullock in-service courses, it is questionable how much other effect the Report had on day-to-day teaching in schools; indeed many of the recommendations are reiterated in Kingman and Cox.

The Kingman Report, while attracting a great deal of media interest, has tended to be overshadowed by the Cox Report and the National Curriculum which followed close behind. However, it is worth considering the recommendations of the Kingman Committee, both for the useful discussion it provides about the teaching of the English language and for the insight it gives into the way thinking was developing about the role of language learning in schools.

The Kingman Committee were given the task by the Government of recommending a model of the English language to act as a basis for teacher training and professional discussion, to consider how far this should be made explicit to pupils in school, and to recommend that children should know of this at the ages of seven, eleven and fourteen. Kingman proposes that language affects all aspects of children's learning: intellectual, social, personal and aesthetic. However, there is evidence of the utilitarian view of language learning that has gained such prominence in the late 1980s. The study of language is said to help children learn to be 'better able to become effective members of a wide range of groups' (p. 10). Similarly, the role of language in personal development is not given such prominence as in Bullock. Although the Report stresses the importance of giving children a wide range of experience of reading and writing in many different forms, it goes on to add, for example, that children who read Tolkien and then write their own fairy stories 'are engaged in a total process of language development which, among other advantages, may one day contribute to the writing of clear, persuasive reports about commerce of science', demonstrating the way the utilitarian view is never far from the authors' minds.

Many of the points made by the Committee provide good advice as to how language should be fostered in school. Particularly that language is best developed through use and reflection rather than by decontextualised analysis. The Report emphasises the way understanding of language can enhance teaching. However, the proposition that knowledge about language aids the learner's progress is not yet proven. Certainly a teacher who is knowledgeable about language can help develop those implicit understandings that children have, but, although the Committee discusses language acquisition, they seem to take little account of these in very young children and ignore the knowledge and resource bilingual speakers bring to the classroom.

Concern for reflection about language leads the Committee to advocate a tentativeness that comes from writing and reading of different types across a range of contexts, and the importance of allowing children to reflect upon their own performance. However, the model of language provided seems to under-value the importance of meaning by placing the emphasis on the form and structure of the language rather than the interpersonal contexts.

The Kingman Report was published in March 1988, and in April the Government set up a working group under the chairmanship of Professor Brian Cox to advise them on appropriate attainment targets and pro- grammes of study for the National Curriculum in English. The first phase for the primary years was to be ready by September, a mere five months from the setting up of the Group. The Cox Report was widely welcomed by teachers, although it must be said more because of a feeling that 'it could have been worse' than for positive reasons. Certainly there is much in it that reflects good practice, but closer examination shows some con- trasting and confusing messages. The main confusion lies in the conflict between what was written in the discussion document and the attainment targets themselves. The Working Group acknowledge the difficulty of defining a linear structure to language learning (DES, 1989b), but accord- ing to their brief requiring them to identify levels of attainment, they had to do just that.

The fact that there were to be only three profile components and six attainment targets (this was later reduced to five when the two for reading were joined together) was welcomed after the complexity and detail of the maths and science documents. However, the fact that the three profile components are split the way they are can lead to compartmentalisation of language teaching which would remove the dynamic of real language use.

There is also a mismatch between the statements about writing and the levels of attainment prescribed. The Working Group state the opinion that the best writing is 'vigorous, committed, honest and interesting' but go on to state that these aspects have not been included in the attainment targets because they cannot be mapped to levels. Where the whole document is considered for discussion, emphasis on language used in context and reinforcement of TGAT's proposition (DES, 1987) that the assessment process should not determine what is taught and learned, puts the levels of attainment into perspective, but where schools plan and teach to the attainment targets there is danger of narrowing the curriculum to the detriment of learners.

The debate and responses to that debate occurred between the publication of the Cox Report in November 1988 and the statutory document for Key Stage One that became law in May 1989 and are now part of history, but it is interesting to consider briefly where the changes occur and what effect they may have on the curriculum.

The first, and most significant change, is the change in order of contents. The placing of the attainment targets at the front of the document reflects views of priorities and is worrying given the Working Group's recommendations that the attainment targets should not lead the curriculum.

Secondly, the programmes of study now encompass all discussion from the original Cox Report about how language should be taught. Hence there is no opportunity to emphasise the Working Group's cautionary remarks about the best ways of learning language. Whilst this leaves teachers free to develop their own methods and beliefs, it can be open to misuse through a narrow interpretation of the attainment targets in particular. In addition there is no longer any mention of bilingual pupils and non-standard English, and drama, media studies and information technology receive only brief mention. This narrows the broad base provided by the Cox Report and ignores valuable sources of learning.

Thirdly, the two attainment targets for reading were combined to form one. Whilst the levels appear to have been amalgamated, an important element has been lost in the reason for the original split. The Working Group recommended that there should be two attainment targets; one concerned with children's intellectual and emotional development and one with special relevance to school and other subjects in the curriculum. This has lessened the value of that personal element by not allowing it to stand in its own right and has truncated the importance of information retrieval in relation to the original content.

Fourthly, the wording of the attainment targets have been tightened up to render them less easy to misinterpret. For example: 'Show a developing sight vocabulary' at Level 1 in reading, of which I heard one teacher say 'There, you see, I can get my flash cards out again', became 'begin to recognise individual words or letters in familiar contexts' which is a more appropriate target than might have been assumed from the earlier statement.

The most important element of the National Curriculum document for the class teacher is the programmes of study. These provide the statutory information about what experience children should receive. It cannot be emphasised too strongly that children who follow the programmes of study should achieve their potential levels in the attainment targets. However, where teachers narrow their focus on to individual statements of level from the attainment targets it is unlikely that children will achieve their potential across the range. Teaching to tests may be successful in the short-term but, if the long-term aim is to achieve literacy in adulthood, a wider range of skills, knowledge and attitudes (which are not included in the attainment targets) should be fostered. Although the discussion in the Cox Report has been shown to reflect contrasting views, the finished document does have a coherence both across the profile components and through the levels of the attainment targets.

In this chapter the content of the National Curriculum for English will be discussed. Strategies teachers might use to facilitate children's progress through this will be discussed in the subsequent chapters.

PROGRAMMES OF STUDY

Reading

Here the emphasis is on the range of experience that children at Key Stage One should receive. Mention is made of 'rich and stimulating texts, both fiction and non-fiction'. The document lists a range of different types of reading matter, both from the type of reading matter that has been traditionally found in infant classrooms and introducing some that are less usual though none the less worthwhile, such as newspapers, maps, computer printout, and other examples from a wide range of reading material. The range should also include children's own writing, tapes, radio, television and home-made books.

Continuity between home and school is seen as important, both in encouraging parents to share in their children's reading and building on the oral language and experiences which children bring from home. Research discussed earlier also stressed the importance of building on children's previous experience. There is recognition that children bring a range of language competencies to the task of learning to read and that reading matter should reflect this. Thus, this variety should be used as a strength and a resource rather than, in some cases, as a 'problem' that needs remediation.

Again, based on the way children learn in the home, reading activities should, where possible, take place in motivating contexts or in the context of play. For example, some reading matter should relate to the 'real' world, books and plays should be written by the children themselves, children should be encouraged to use information books in response to questions that they themselves have raised. There is emphasis on encouraging children to talk about the reading that they have done, with the teacher and each other. This should include discussion about stories and information books, the motives of characters in stories, alternative endings, whether they enjoyed a particular text and why, and the way in which language is written down. There should also be provision for children to hear stories, poems etc. read aloud by the teacher and each other.

It is expected that children will be encouraged to become independent, autonomous readers. This, of course, is essential if they are to continue to use their skill in the future. This also follows the research discussed earlier which showed that children learn best if they are actively involved in what they are doing. Children are expected to be able to choose what they would like to read or hear read and to give opinions on this. Since children are to formulate their own questions about information texts and to discuss these as well, it follows that they will learn to be discerning about the appropriateness of such texts. The discussion that will take place will encourage them to become reflective readers, able to choose reading matter for pleasure and to find information.

Also detailed is precise information about what children should be taught about reading. This is in addition to the range of experiences provided that are described above and will be achieved both by the teacher modelling the process and by teaching that is targeted upon those children who are at the appropriate stage. No information is given as to how this should be done but it is left to the experience of teachers and to books such as this to suggest strategies. That which is to be taught covers the purpose and use of reading, the whole range of strategies used by the reader, the ability to read aloud competently and also to read silently.

Writing

The programmes of study are organised according to profile components and not attainment targets; therefore the three attainment targets for writing are taken together. The same strands can be followed through the programmes of study for writing: the range of provision, use of literacy contexts from within the child's experience both inside and outside school, building on children's previous experience, the importance of discussion, and the development of independence and autonomy.

There is the same emphasis on experience of a range of writing contexts, both chronological and non-chronological kinds of writing and including such things as posters, plans, diagrams etc. Again there is the stress on building on the children's own experience of language, for instance awareness of mother tongue writing systems where appropriate and opportunities to produce examples of written text such as they would see in the home: birthday cards, invitations, letters etc. In the same way there should be the chance for children to write for real purposes and a variety of audiences producing many of the types of writing that are seen in the world outside school. It is often suggested that these opportunities will arise through the context of play.

The opportunity for children to talk about the writing they have done is again stressed. They should write individually and in groups, discuss their writing frequently, and learn about grammatical terms *in the context of discussion*. Also, as with reading, they should have the opportunity to see adults writing. Teachers are expected to write alongside their pupils, sharing and talking about their writing.

There is less emphasis on developing independent, autonomous writers than there is with reading. They should be given the chance to compose at greater length than they can write by dictation, working with peers or using a word-processor. They should also be encouraged to spell words for themselves. It is only at Level 3 that pupils are required to start to recognise that writing involves decision making and planning, and that they should be encouraged to make choices and judgements about their writing.

In the programmes of study for writing there is more indication given as to what should be taught. Children need to be taught ways of forming letter shapes through *purposeful, guided practice*. They should be introduced to common spelling patterns, and the names and order of the letters of the alphabet. They also need to be taught to leave spaces between words and to use simple punctuation correctly. Interestingly, there is mention of teaching metalanguage at this stage for writing but not for reading, although the metalanguage of reading is possibly more important for any discussion of texts. The same emphases are also evident in the programmes of study for speaking and listening, although it is not the intention to discuss these here. So a picture emerges of a classroom which provides a range of literacy experiences based on a variety of literacy contexts including ones from the world outside school in which the children are encouraged to take an active part. Children will be given opportunities to discuss their literacy endeavours and to begin to develop strategies for independence in use of literacy. In addition to the exciting range of experiences provided by the teacher, there will also be input from the teacher. This will include a modelling of the processes involved, teaching about elements essential to literacy learning that the child does not pick up for him/herself (which vary from child to child), and assessment by the teacher of the progress made by children in order that provision for individuals is appropriate.

LEVELS OF ATTAINMENT

The way these programmes of study are reflected by the statements of levels of the attainment targets shows a concern for the same underlying principles. This is represented in diagrammatic form in Table 2. However, particularly in the attainment targets for writing, there is more emphasis on the surface structure than is implied in the programmes of study. This takes us back to the statement from the Cox Report in which

Table 2 *Relationship between programmes of study and attainment targets*

Principles behind POS	AT 2	AT 3	AT 4	AT 5
1 Range of experience	1 a, b			
	2 a, e, f	2 b, c, d		
	3 a, f	3 b, c, d		
2 Contexts from children's own experience of real world	1 a, b			
	2 a			
	3 a, d			
3 Importance of discussion	1 d			
	2 d, e			
	3 c, d, e	3 e		
4 Development of autonomy	1 c		1 c	
	2 e, f	2 a	2 a, c	
	3 b, d, f	3 a, e	3 d	

the Working Group recognises that the best writing is vigorous, committed, honest and interesting – qualities which have not been included in the statements of attainment as they cannot be mapped on to levels. How important, then, it is for teachers to follow the programmes of study in order to give children the opportunity to develop their writing to its full potential?

The need for a range of experience is emphasised in the statements for reading and at Levels 2 and 3 in Attainment Target 3. It is implicit in the attainment target for spelling that correct spelling should be found in the course of the child's own writing. Handwriting refers only to the formation of letters, but it seems unlikely that assessment will be on the writing of individual letters rather than on a selection from the writing samples from the child. The statements related to writing give less explanation about the contexts for writing than those related to reading. Types of writing are divided into stories, chronological and non-chronological writing, and it is left up to the teacher to go to the programmes of study to find examples of these. There is far greater emphasis on reading material from the everyday world in the statements for reading, although the programmes of study for writing do stress the importance of experiencing writing contexts from the 'real' world.

The importance of discussion is very evident in the statements on reading, but only gets mention at Level 3 in writing. However, earlier examination of the way children learn has shown that interaction plays a crucial role, so, more than ever, the programmes of study indicate the teaching and learning contexts.

The development of independent, autonomous literacy users is evident in the three attainment targets (again, the type of statements made for handwriting refer only to the formation of letters, presumably in the course of their writing). In reading, children are assessed according to their ability to show interest in reading, give opinions on what they have read, read independently, go beyond literal meanings, and use their reading to find information. In writing, at Level 1, they should be able to produce attempts at words (single letters or groups of letters to represent words) to communicate meaning. By Level 2 they are expected to be able to produce writing independently and to make attempts at spelling that show they can make use of their knowledge and understanding even if they are not necessarily correct. This obviously has implications for the classroom, in that it will not be appropriate for children to be expected to learn to write only by copying sentences first and later any word that they are not confident to spell correctly on their own. There will have to be a tentativeness that may result in error in children's work, but more of this later. The introduction of revising and redrafting at Level 3 necessitates that children can begin to check their own writing.

How a child at each level might look will be examined later but, at this point, the progression through the levels can be examined. Some statements are clear as to the standard required whereas others mention 'a wider range' and 'some control' which are harder to interpret and will require experience and moderation.

Reading

The reader moves from understanding that print carries meaning and recognising individual words and letters in contexts, through reading with 'some independence, fluency, accuracy and understanding', to reading familiar material fluently and with expression. The strategies used by the child in his/her reading development are described as moving from recognition of individual letters or words at Level 1, to using picture, context and phonic cues at Level 2. By Level 3 they are beginning to develop skills of comprehension such as recall of significant detail, inference etc., and also to read silently. At Level 1, children will show an interest in reading, at Level 2, be able to listen and respond to stories and to predict what might happen next, and by Level 3, understand and discuss the way stories are structured, including setting, characters and meanings beyond the literal.

Thus the young reader is expected to develop the ability to reflect on what he/she has read. At Level 1 this might include saying what parts of the story or information text they have liked. At Level 2 these opinions should be more directly informed by what has been read and include the ability to predict what may happen next. At Level 3 this is extended and includes the detail referred to in the previous paragraph. Accuracy is introduced at Level 2 for the reading of signs, labels and notices and children are expected to demonstrate knowledge of the alphabet. By Level 3 they should be able to read aloud familiar material with fluency and expression. Children are expected to use non-fiction books as well as fiction from Level 1, and by Level 3 they should be able to decide for themselves what information they might want to find in these and know how to locate it.

It is interesting to consider that there is far greater emphasis on reflection, comprehension and use of reading than has traditionally been the case with children of this age where accurate reading of limited texts was the norm for the learner.

Writing

In order to examine development through Levels 1 and 2, the progress of the young writer through the levels of the National Curriculum will be illustrated by examples from Lee's first seven terms in school. Lee is a child of average ability (insofar as it is possible to describe a child as such), who started school in the summer term of 1988.

As has been indicated earlier, the statements of attainment relating to writing place more emphasis on surface structure than expression. There is very little detail given in Attainment Target 3 as to how the beginning writer will develop before Level 2 which is somewhat surprising, given the work undertaken as part of the National Writing Project which has shown just how much children do know about writing at the early stages. The child at Level 1 will be able to make symbols to represent meaning whereas the child at Level 2 can sequence and structure chronological and non-chronological writing and produce this using complete sentences with some use of capital letters and full stops. While this wide interval between levels 1 and 2 is helpful if it allows the child time to experiment, direct 'cramming' towards Level 2 could result in children developing an incomplete idea of written language if production of pieces of writing is hurried at the expense of understanding.

The account of development between Levels 2 and 3 is not very clearly defined. For example, children move from using 'some' sentences with capital letters and full stops to having them 'mainly' demarcated in this way. Similarly Level 3 requires children to develop their understanding of the way writing is structured and to demonstrate this in a more complex way than at Level 2, increasing the range of models of writing and including more detail. Also, as previously mentioned, Level 3 sees the introduction of revising and redrafting.

Lee, on starting school, wrote symbols to represent meaning, at first without using sentences *'Footballs'* (May, 1988). He could also dictate a more complex sentence *'Every time I go out I run away from big dogs'* (September 1988). As he progresses his writing becomes more varied:

'I like the walk because it was good we heard a dog barking' (February, 1989)

'I always have breakfast. I always have jam on my toast' (November, 1989)

'I like to play American football with my brother and I can make touchdowns' (May, 1990)

'On Monday I went to Sidmouth beach with my sister and her friend Alison and then we went to the pub I went to the play park and then I went to

Bicton Park and I went on the ghost train and the rifles and the maze and a motor bike and Bash the Gophers and a computer (June, 1990)

Thus, two years from starting school Lee's writing has developed and he can now write both chronological and non-chronological kinds of writing. He writes in sentences but has not yet learned to demarcate these with full stops and capital letters.

The young speller is expected to develop correctness gradually. At Level 1 he/she shows some ability to match sound to symbol, by Level 2 is able to spell a range of simple, monosyllabic words, and by Level 3 simple, polysyllabic words both of which have a regular pattern. Also at Level 2 the expectation is that common words should be spelt in a recognisable (though not necessarily always correct) way.

The development of sound symbol correspondence is also gradual, from writing some letter shapes in response to speech sounds, to the correct spelling of monosyllabic words, to polysyllabic words and regular vowel sounds and letter strings at Level 3. The development of strategies for spelling is an important factor of the statements of attainment and has more emphasis than either correctness or the development of memory which have traditionally been stressed in infant classrooms. Thus, at Level 1 the beginning writer is shown to be tentative and concerned with communicating meaning through whatever means he/she has available, i.e. using letters or groups of letters to represent words. The tentativeness continues into Level 2 in which common words should be spelt correctly, and children are expected to show that they understand that spelling has patterns and to use this knowledge in 'their attempts' to spell other words. Also at Level 2 they have to know the names and order of the letters of the alphabet, knowledge that can only be useful for finding words from dictionaries and talking to others about spelling, stressing again the development of strategies for independence. At Level 3 children are expected to spell correctly words following regular patterns and those containing vowel sounds and common letter strings. In the spelling of more complex or less familiar words they should show awareness of word families and relationships, i.e. use the strategies they have been taught or have gleaned from their own reading and writing. Also at this level they are expected to demonstrate their independence by checking the accuracy of their spelling while revising and redrafting.

Lee, when he started school, was not at Level 1; he produced a mixture of symbols, letters shapes and numbers.

After a year he is able to produce some recognisable spellings and knows a few monosyllabic words:

'*I wod like to do the 3 lagd ras*' (July, 1989)

and is beginning to apply his knowledge of patterns of spelling in his attempts at words: '*brcing*' – barking (February, 1989). This ability continues to develop and, by summer 1990, he can spell many words correctly: '*Monday, went, with, my, sister, play, and*'; and make some good attempts at others: '*tuchdaoons*' – touchdowns, '*biech*' – beach, '*trane*' – train (June, 1990).

Attainment Target 5, for handwriting, describes the development of legible and tidy writing. The young writer moves from being expected to have some control over shape, size and orientation, to correct and consistent use of these. These statements are straightforward, but give no indication of how these will be achieved and teachers will decide for themselves whether copy writing assists in progress towards these levels. The inclusion of cursive writing at Level 3 has implications for schools that had not previously introduced this until well into the juniors. Cursive writing is introduced by a small minority of schools from the reception class, although it would seem difficult to encourage cursive writing from the beginning as well as developing an awareness of the way print is found all around in the everyday world.

Lee in his short time at school has moved from:

through:

to:

However, in handwriting, he is still at Level 1. Although his writing is legible with most letters correctly formed and oriented, he is not using either lower or upper case consistently and correct use of ascenders and descenders is sporadic.

CONCLUSION

This chapter has discussed how recent HMI and Government initiatives have focused attention on the learning of literacy with a concern that education should produce adults who can not only perform the mechanical skills of reading and writing but be able to use their knowledge of literacy for pleasure and to meet the challenges of the adult world today.

Consideration of the National Curriculum has demonstrated how the document reflects both the research that has been described in the first three chapters of this book and also the public concern described above. It has been shown how provision for literacy learning is expected to be based on children's own experience and set in authentic contexts wherever possible. The range of contexts for reading and writing is also seen to be important at Key Stage One which implies a move from a philosophy that caused teachers to believe that children need to be taught the skills of reading and writing before they could use them. The value of discussion in learning is also evident in both the programmes of study and the statements of levels of attainment, reflecting theories of learning that stress the importance of interaction. The concern for developing autonomous, independent learners and users of literacy is also very evident, preparing the child for a lifetime of learning and pleasure not merely the achievement of a narrow range of qualifications at the end of formal schooling.

The attention now turns to the role of the teacher in the achievement of these goals. The roles to be described emerge from evidence discussed in the earlier chapters from research into literacy learning, the child, the teacher and the National Curriculum. A picture emerges of a teacher with an important and specific role to play. Someone who is far more than a didactic figure imparting knowledge, and more again than only a facilitator who expects learning to take place from no more than the provision of a stimulating environment and some good books. The teacher is someone who can facilitate learning by the range of provision in the classroom; one who can lead a child to an understanding of the task by modelling attitudes and behaviour that are crucial to lasting development; one who can manage the learning situation in order to enable children to achieve their potential; and, most importantly, one who can observe and assess children's performance in order to ensure that the other roles work effectively for the individual child.

5 The teacher as facilitator

The roles to be examined in this book are those of facilitator, model, manager of learning, and assessor. It has been shown how teachers, responding to criticisms in the press and conflicting ideologies of early years education find themselves walking an 'ideological tightrope' (Alexander, 1988). Each of the roles examined here allows teachers to identify their part in the teaching of literacy and is supported by an interactionist and constructivist view of learning. These roles acknowledge the child to be an active participant in the learning process with the adult supporting and enabling the child's development. There is no in-built hierarchy intended in the presentation of the roles, rather they should be seen as being of equal importance; interrelated and interdependent.

The child at Key Stage One has been seen to be a lively, active being who is both willing and able to learn. Indeed the child on starting compulsory schooling has already gathered a great deal of knowledge about the world in which he/she lives. It has also been shown that the teacher's role is crucial in the development of children's learning after entering school. Thus it is the task of the teacher to build upon the knowledge children already have and to enable them to continue to learn. The teacher's role is to facilitate progress in learning. This he/she does by making decisions; decisions about the environment provided for the children, about the resources chosen, and about the context within which the learning takes place. In addition, the teacher will facilitate or hinder learning according to the response made to the child.

It is these aspects of the teacher's role that will be considered in this chapter. A further chapter will examine the role of the teacher as manager in which questions of how time can best be used to enable the sort of context described below to occur. It is too often the case that books describe an ideal situation that seems far-reached from the day-to-day life with a class of thirty plus five- and six-year-olds.

MAKING DECISIONS

At the beginning of a new year, new term, new day and many times during the day the teacher must make decisions. These involve decisions about the environment within the classroom, what to have in and what to leave out, whether the area is best used to give children a seat of their own or whether priority should be given to reading corners, writing areas and other dedicated space. Money spent at a time of reduced budgets and greater accountability must be used to its best effect, therefore thought has to be given as to what books should be bought, and whether money should be spent on a series of worksheets or some expensive but superior picture books. The infant classroom no longer keeps the door closed to other people and the infant teacher must make decisions about the use of people as a resource.

The National Curriculum has brought some clarity to the expectations of what children should be able to do at certain ages but little statutory guidance is given as to how this should be achieved. The teacher is still left with decisions to make about the learning context. Much emphasis is placed on relevance and audience within the non-statutory guidelines and decisions must be made about how this can be brought about. Children are expected to be allowed to experiment and to develop their own strategies for reading and writing in order to develop a good understanding of the task. Evidence shows that classes where there is a wide range of language activities offered to the children make better progress (see Table 1 on page 51). Thus, there are more decisions to be made about the learning context than if it were simply thought to be enough to invest in a good reading scheme with phonic support.

THE CLASSROOM ENVIRONMENT

1 The reading corner

The Primary (DES, 1978) and First School (DES, 1982a) Surveys reported that schools did not have available to children a wide range of non-scheme reading material. This has changed and few infant classrooms can now be found where there is not a collection of books for children to read. However, the quality of these areas is variable. The sort of decisions that teachers must make about the establishment or improvement of an area like this involve answers to the following questions:

What reading matter should I include?
How can that material be best displayed?
When can children have access to this area?
Where and how should they read?
How can I make the area inviting?
Is it appropriate for the teacher to become involved?

The answers made to these questions will be guided by our knowledge of the way in which children learn, the task of learning about literacy and procedures for achieving effective classroom practice. Thus the child will be viewed as an active learner, who already has some knowledge of the reading process. Reading will be seen as an enjoyable, creative process which is undertaken for a wide range of purposes which are understood by the reader. The classroom will be taken as an arena within which children will have opportunities to make decisions, to try out ideas, make mistakes, to learn and to be taught.

What reading matter should I include?
The area under discussion is often called 'the book corner' and is just that. However, thought about the environment of today's world will show that books are only a part of what we choose to read. If we want children to develop the ability to relate their reading behaviour to life outside of school and if we want them to learn to exercise choice in their reading material, it is important to encourage and allow that choice.

A reading corner should include books, of course, but also catalogues, directories (children love telephone directories – what other book contains their name and address!), comics, magazines, newspapers, leaflets, brochures and anything else that relates to the children's life and interests. Teachers are often wary of including items such as comics in a classroom, but, whilst they certainly are open to criticism on a number of grounds, they do encourage some children to read when they have little interest in other reading matter. The argument is similar to that against banning Enid Blyton – if children can start to enjoy reading through these books the teacher can provide experience of more sophisticated texts which most children will soon want to explore for themselves. The reading corner will certainly also contain reading matter related to the other areas of the curriculum. Literacy is not taught in isolation but in all contexts where it is genuinely used.

Books will of course be the major component of a reading corner – fiction books, information books, picture books, big books, difficult books, easy books – variety being an essential component in encouraging choice and interest. In whatever area of the country the school is situated a reading area should include examples of different languages. This is relevant whether to enlarge the monolingual child's knowledge of other languages and incidently extend their understanding to their own, or whether to provide interest and enhancement of self-esteem for bi- or multilingual children in the classroom.

How can that material be best displayed?
Young children cannot be expected to be experienced enough readers to pick books from their spines, they need to be able to see the cover and to reach them for themselves. If the development of independence and critical choice is seen to be important, access to the reading matter is crucial. Shelving that allows the book to be seen easily, to be picked up

and, of equal importance, to be put back without damage. Posters about authors and books, pictures or models or characters from the books also make the area an attractive and interesting reading environment.

When can children have access to this area?
It is frequently the case that children are 'given permission' to use a reading area when they have finished a prescribed task. The unfortunate result of this can be that the children who have most access to the reading corner are those who are already high achievers, whilst those who find the tasks set either uninteresting or difficult do not get the opportunity to browse amongst the books. Yet it is often these children who have most need for these opportunities. If time spent in the reading area is taken to be an important part of the child's day, this should be built into every child's routine.

Where and how should they read?
The Schools Council Project *Extending Beginning Reading* (Southgate *et al.* 1981) recommended a time of sustained silent reading on books of their own choice for all seven-to-nine-year-old children (and teachers) each day. This has been introduced into a few National Curriculum Year Two classes with some success. However, silence is not easy for young children and, remembering the importance of interaction in learning, talk can be considered to be an important part of the child's experience of reading. Some children will choose to read silently and on their own on some occasions and others will want to share their reading with a friend or an adult. Children enjoy taking on the role of the teacher and reading a story to another child or group of children. These behaviours should be encouraged in that they allow children to explore the concept of reading and to develop their own particular preferences.

In the same way it is unrealistic to expect that children will always read sitting up (I certainly do not). Cushions, covered boxes, carpet to lie on as well as chairs should be available for them to choose.

How can I make the area inviting?
The variety of seating described above can be bought or made quite cheaply and covered in comfortable, attractive material. Posters, pictures and models related to the reading matter on display add interest. Books that have recently been read to the class, if prominently displayed, often provide a focus of attention for those less experienced in choosing books for themselves. Some measure of privacy is also desirable in that it can help concentration and motivate children to use the area. Cupboards at

right angles to the wall, hanging drapes and corrugated card can create an interesting and private area.

Is it appropriate for the teacher to become involved?
Whilst children do need time to explore reading in their own way and without intervention on the part of the teacher, children are different and, while some children like to spend time near to the teacher, others are happy to work more independently. Similarly, activities that are judged to be valued by the teacher will be valued in turn by the children. Thus it is important for the teacher to show his/her interest and appreciation of the activities chosen by the children.

An area of the size of a reading corner is also likely to be used by the teacher for teaching opportunities when appropriate; working with individuals and small groups and for the informal assessment of individuals.

2 The writing area

A reading corner may be considered an essential part of the infant classroom, but writing areas are less common. The work of the National Writing Project has had an important effect on the way young children are taught to write and opportunities for them to explore the writing process are now seen to be advantageous. The non-statutory guidance also promotes the idea of children practising and experimenting with newly learned skills.

The first decision to be made is often where to put a writing area in an already crowded classroom. Space and opportunity to write is the main criterion and this can be provided by a writing box if no space is available for a table or work surface. The box could contain all the equipment that would be in a writing area but it could be taken by the child to any space that was available at that time.

Similar questions to those posed in the design of a reading area are relevant in this case also:

What should the area contain?
When should children have access to it?
How can it be made inviting?
How should children be expected to use it?
Is it appropriate for the teacher to intervene?

The answers to these questions, as those above, will be guided by our knowledge of children and of the process involved. Thus the writing area will include a variety of material to write with and on: a range of shape, size and quality of paper; forms, cards, wipe-clean boards, etc., and pens, pencils, crayons of different colour and thickness.

Children should have choice of access to the area as routine for all children and should be allowed to use it freely. There will be plenty of opportunities for children to have their writing judged by the teacher, so the free writing that children choose to do for themselves should not need to be examined and judged unless that is the child's choice. Emphasis in the National Curriculum is on experimentation and allowing learners to explore the processes for themselves in order to learn and understand rules. It is often difficult to bestow on children the confidence to experiment since they can have been made only too aware of the shortfall between their efforts and correct adult writing. Free writing can enable children to explore spelling patterns, handwriting style and modes of expression without fear or failure. In the same way as for the reading corner, teachers should also show that they value the activities undertaken by the children. This can be done by showing interest and appreciation of the writing produced by the children and by writing themselves when appropriate.

3 Play areas

The value of play in the early years of education is widely recognised and structured provision for infants can be found in many classrooms, yet it is often the case that reading and writing is not deemed an appropriate part of this. However, both reading and writing play such an important part in everyday life that this should be reflected in play situations. A variety of role-play areas can be found in many infant classrooms: home corner, café, doctor's surgery, travel agent and many others. These all present ample and real opportunities for children to explore the purposes of reading and writing as well as aspects of social life and learning in other curriculum areas. Home corners usually centre around a kitchen-type room, yet few of these reflect the amount of written material there would normally be in the average home: circulars, recipe books, notice boards, TV/Radio Times, newspapers, instruction booklets for cookers etc., labels, shopping lists and many more elements of everyday life. Other types of imaginative play area also provide a range of contexts for children to explore reading and writing: filling in forms, making appointments, choosing holidays, reading notices, finding and recording information and so on. This also answers some of those teachers who claim that imaginative play is no longer appropriate for Year Two children – they did it in the reception class. Structure by means of variety and differing opportunities can render this type of play as important for seven-year-olds as it was for four- and five-year-olds.

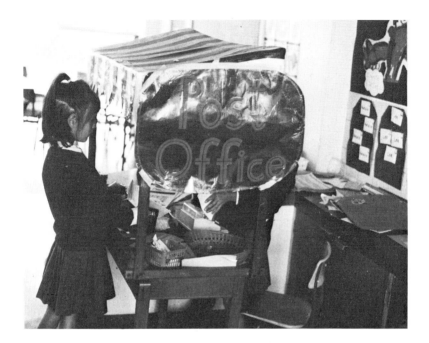

DECISIONS ABOUT RESOURCES

1 Published books

The teacher has, now more than ever, to be an expert on many things. One area in which informed knowledge is important is in the books that are available for children to read. In the last few years the number of good books that have been written for children has grown enormously and it would be impossible to do justice to the range and scope of these in a couple of pages. However, there are various principles that can be applied to the choice of books which it is appropriate to discuss here, and there are many useful publications such as *Books for Keeps* and *Books for Children* which can help keep teachers up to date with the numerous publications.

The question 'What makes a good book?' essentially has to be answered subjectively, but Margaret Meek's booklet *How Texts Teach what Readers Learn* (1988) gives some guidance as to what might be of benefit to children who are learning about the process of reading. She identifies the 'untaught lessons' of books.

1   How the book works and the way stories go.

2   The way the reader interacts with the text, for example the fact that the fox is not mentioned anywhere in the text in *Rosie's Walk* by Pat Hutchins. Meek writes 'It is a lesson we take with us from wherever we first learned it to our understanding of Jane Austin'.

3   Metaphor, in other words the fact that words can mean more than their face value.

4   The nature and variety of discourse.

5   That texts are polysemic, with use of allusion and intertext as in, for example, *The Jolly Postman* by the Ahlbergs.

6   The content of the story and the way different value systems are reflected in the text.

Thus, the 'good' book for children, as well as for adults, is one that can be interpreted on a variety of levels and that can be revisited time and again with new interest and discovery. In books for young children this is often achieved through partnership between author and illustrator, where the two aspects of the text link together to enhance the whole.

In addition to considerations about quality, range and variety is also important because of the subjective nature of our judgements. Not all children will find the same books appealing and there should be sufficient choice for them firstly to discover where their preferences lie and secondly to find books that are to their choosing. Thus, there should be information books, picture books, pop-up books, books in rhyme, poetry books, factual books, fiction books, books that are easy to read, books with no print, books that are too hard for most of the children but that may still offer something to particular children; the list could go on and on to reflect a full range.

2 Teacher and child-made books

All schools will work within a limited budget and money available will have to be spent carefully. For this reason and because of their intrinsic value, home-produced books should not be forgotten. These have the advantage of relevance to the reader, the fact that the reader has been involved in some way in the process, and may even star in the text. These books can include compilations of children's work, text written by the teacher, by a child or children (from the class or from another class) in various languages if appropriate, photographs with text, children's illustrations either produced or chosen by them. These books can be presented attractively and are undoubtedly a great favourite with children.

These present tremendous opportunities for children to learn about the links between reading and writing. In no way can the concept be made more real than by enabling children to go through the whole process from initial idea, through production to publication.

3 Environmental print

Chapter 2 discussed how children bring to school some knowledge and experience to print and that this should be built upon. The range of material to be found in the classroom should reflect this. Children from their first term in school will enjoy producing shopping lists, writing letters, and making an advertisement – for many children these may be more genuine tasks than writing a story or a piece of 'news' as they will represent a part of the life they know. By National Curriculum Year Two, newspapers, comics, school brochures, signs, labels, instructions should all be part of what children read and write.

4 Teaching materials

Computer programs, flip-over charts, white/black boards, flannel graphs, alphabet boards, message boards, *Breakthrough to Literacy* teachers' stands (which provide ready-made printed words and a stand to hold them, and can be used to demonstrate the flexibility of language and introduce some aspects of metalanguage) video and audio tapes all provide good opportunities for children to experiment and teachers to demonstrate aspects of literacy.

It is not the intention here to discuss the range of published teaching materials available and how desirable they might be. The argument has been rehearsed earlier and, to a certain extent, is irrelevant here. The teacher as facilitator will choose whatever resources he/she feels is appropriate to his/her class. However, if the child is considered to be an active learner who already has some knowledge of the task and who is learning to use something that is relevant to him/her as an individual, many schemes which follow a distant publisher's agenda rather than the agenda of the child will not be deemed appropriate. In the same way the teacher who believes that the child learns best when tasks are part of a wider context and make sense to the child is not likely to choose a worksheet or page from a book which concentrates on one particular skill. With the breadth and volume of curriculum to be covered, it is difficult to see how many isolated English lessons would be possible, even if they were desirable. The importance of learning literacy within a wider context assists the teacher trying to cover the content of the whole National Curriculum as well as the child who learns better when the learning is in context.

5 People as a resource

The non-statutory guidance puts people as the first resource in its review of resources, and certainly the infant classroom today is no longer the closed room that it was some years ago. The National Curriculum and the kinds of learning programme described in this book require a large amount of interaction between adult and child and this is one reason why the inclusion of other adults in the classroom is valuable. However, this is not the only reason. The value of involving parents in the process of learning literacy is emphasised in the Programme of Study 9, and is also one of the elements identified by several of the studies discussed in Chapter 3, and certainly parental involvement in the teaching of reading projects has evidenced some success. However, evidence has shown that in order for the parental involvement to be successful it should be established on rather a more personal basis than the ubiquitous PTA (Mortimore et al., 1988: ILEA, 1988) and involve careful organisation and interaction with the parents (Tizard et al., 1988).

Adults and older children in the classroom can provide a good way of freeing the beginning writers from the mechanics of the writing process, thereby allowing them to practise expression in written language without the slowing effect of inadequate ability in spelling and handwriting and thus providing them with the opportunity to 'compose at greater length than they can write' (DES, 1989b, POS 18).

In addition, since the child has been shown to be a successful learner in the home where the contexts make sense to him/her, people invited in from the home community to talk to children, work with them, tell stories, share books, sing songs and teach traditional rhymes and stories in English and other mother tongues, can often be in a better position than the teacher to make connections between past and future experience and the literacy experience of the classroom for children. The research reported in Chapter 2 (Brice Heath, 1982) showed that many children came to school with different experiences of literacy and that these were not always built upon in the classroom. Involvement of the community in classroom practice can extend the range of experience given to children and maybe lessen the alienation experienced by some children.

Tape-recorders and word processors present other ways of enabling children to experiment with written language whilst avoiding some aspects of the mechanical elements.

DECISIONS ABOUT THE LEARNING CONTEXT

The programmes of study and non-statutory guidance for the National Curriculum emphasise the importance of contextualising the language work that is undertaken by children. The reason for this has been clearly seen in Chapter 2 where the way children learn was considered. In the previous sections there has been discussion of the ways in which the teacher can facilitate this by providing a range of literacy experience in the classroom that mirrors the uses of literacy in society, and in learning throughout the curriculum.

Equally important is the way in which the children are expected to undertake the activity. No longer are they expected to be passive recipients of instruction but are required to take an active part in the learning process. This is achieved in a number of ways: choice, opinion, opportunities to construct meaning, and experimentation.

Choice

Some approaches to the teaching of reading and writing do not introduce very much choice; writing being in response to the demands of the teacher and the reading book chosen according to the published scheme rather than the need of the child. One outcome of this could be that children do not learn how to choose, or even that choice is a part of expected literacy behaviour. When the reading scheme is finished and the children are allowed to choose, they have no strategies to do this and often no incentive because the driving force of getting on to the next book of the scheme is lost. The element of choice is not mentioned in the National Curriculum attainment targets but choice is evident in the programmes of study and must surely be an essential ingredient in an efficient adult reader. In addition, choice can provide children with the opportunity to experiment with writing and reading in ways that make sense to them and which will help to develop an understanding of the process.

Choice, however, will need to be monitored. Inappropriate choice is the concern of many teachers that children may consistently choose books that do not challenge their ability as readers or, conversely, which are beyond their ability to understand without help. Choice involves freedom to choose what is read, when and how; similarly what is written when and how. This does not imply that all reading and writing will be left to the free choice of the child. The teacher will need to give children a wide range of experience in reading and writing, such as those described in this chapter and in the programmes of study for the National Curriculum, so that they have a repertoire from which to make choices.

Opinion

Opinion is an element that is included in the National Curriculum, and in both reading and writing, children are expected to be able to talk about what they have written and what they have read, to express opinions informed by this (AT 2 Level 2) and to make judgements upon their own writing (AT 3 Level 3).

The programmes of study place a heavy emphasis on the importance of talking about reading and writing. In the past some teacher- or publisher-directed schemes have not allowed for children's opinion. Motivation was provided extrinsically by the desire to get on to the next book or worksheet, and the child was not expected to pass opinion on the books read. Teachers, with every good intention, encouraged a love of books and this could sometimes become the love of every book supplied by the school without regard for individual preference. With the current explosion in the number of good books written for children, it is a pleasure to read with even the youngest children in the school and to hear their opinions of the authors, texts and storyline. Evidence has shown that poor readers find it difficult to assess whether a text makes sense or not and tend to assume that the fault lies with their reading rather than with the text itself (Garner, 1987). Encouraging children to discuss what they are reading will engender a healthy critical attitude which will stand them in good stead throughout their reading career. This does not have to be limited to opinions about books, but also to newspaper articles or advertising material (when they relate to the child's own experience).

Discussion about published texts can lead to discussion about the children's own written language. Children enjoy the opportunity to say what they like about another child's writing and to ask questions about it. When this type of 'conferencing' is modelled by the teacher in a positive way, children themselves provide positive reinforcement to their peers. When the only comment about writing that is known is that it is untidy, poorly spelt or not long enough, these will be the comments made. Peer conferencing can also lead on to self-assessment which is a valuable element in the assessment of learners.

Opportunities to construct meaning

Chapter 2 showed children to be active learners who are constantly constructing meaning for themselves. If they are allowed to use this capacity in their literacy learning they will learn all the more effectively. To do this appropriately the uses they make of literacy should be relevant and purposeful. Work undertaken by the National Writing Project showed how providing children with an audience for their writing assisted both their confidence and competence. The programme of study for writing emphasises the importance of children having frequent opportunities to write for a variety of purposes and audiences.

Occasions for writing and reading occur in every aspect of life and these opportunities can be offered in the classroom. Letter boxes, message boards, lists, instructions, records, class diaries are all opportunities for children to use writing in a way that makes sense to them and to construct their own meanings in a relevant context.

Experimentation

Learning in all areas of endeavour involves experimentation and error, so it is surprising that some traditional methods of teaching reading and writing have required children to produce word-perfect efforts from the beginning. Many of the studies of effective classroom practice emphasise the importance of a degree of tolerance for error and the encouragement for children to find their own solutions to problems (see Table 1 on page 51). This does not refer only to literacy learning but is certainly important in many contexts. However, not only has this been shown to be effective educational practice, but it also frees the teacher to allow time to be spent working with other children; few things are more time-consuming in the infant classroom than giving words.

Allied to this is the issue of a sense of ownership, particularly of writing. Where children are allowed some measure of choice in the literacy activities they undertake, can express valued opinions about literacy experiences and are encouraged to actively construct meaning in their use of literacy, they will develop a sense that these activities are of relevance and interest to them which should provide intrinsic motivation for further development.

This is particularly important in the development of written style and interpretation of texts, but it is also part of learning to spell. The need for the teacher to encourage children to try out their spellings before asking or looking them up was evidenced by Peters (1970). In the National Curriculum, Level 2 of Attainment Target 4 requires children to be able to make recognisable attempts at words and to apply knowledge from one set of words to the spelling of another. To do this successfully children will have to have the confidence to take chances without fear of censure if their attempts are incorrect. In addition, one aspect of spelling that has been neglected in the early teaching of spelling is the ability to recognise error. Thus, children who are always given the correct spelling if they are unsure and always have their spelling errors identified by the teacher have not developed strategies for judging their own attempts and become over-reliant on the teacher.

Children should learn to develop strategies that will remain with them through schooling and into adult life. Thus, the teacher's role is to encourage experimentation followed, as the child gains confidence and competence, by identification of errors *by the child*. The teacher's role is also to explain skills to enable word retrieval, advocate the use of strategies to develop visual memory of spellings, such as 'look, cover, write, check' and to explain and encourage the use of sound-symbol correspondence when appropriate.

The opportunity to self-correct is also important in reading. Good readers have been shown to self-correct when subsequent lines reveal their mistakes; poor readers on the other hand seem to be less able to do this (Clay, 1979) and thus have difficulty with comprehension. If the child can be allowed to read on past the error and is then questioned about what he/she has read, the ability to judge the sense of his/her interpretation will have a chance to develop.

RESPONSE

In addition to making decisions about the learning context, the teacher will facilitate learning by the responses made to the child. To consider this aspect it is necessary in the first place to examine the opportunities for interaction in the classroom. In Chapter 2 it was shown how interaction plays a crucial part in the child's learning, and Chapter 3 provided evidence from studies of effective classrooms as to the importance of a high level of interaction. Wells (1981) demonstrates the difference between interaction in the home and interaction between adult and child in school, to the detriment of the latter. He identifies areas of difference and demonstrates how the style of interaction effects the quality of learning.

Opportunities for a high quality of interaction arise in classrooms when these are a planned part of the agenda and when the teacher's management enables these to occur. Interaction can occur between child and teacher, another adult and child, and child and child. Each is valuable when planned and provided for as part of the management of the school day. Contexts for interaction within literacy learning are many. For example: discussion of stories read to or by the child, discussion of writing undertaken by the child or adult, examination of various forms of print in the environment, the discussion of information sought or found by the child, and many others.

In order for the interaction between adult and child to be of a high level there are several prerequisites which are the responsibility of the adult to provide:

- quality of relationship;
- opportunity for the child to be the expert;
- tolerance of error; and
- the ability to listen.

Quality of relationship

Language learning takes place in the home in an atmosphere of close, emotional relationships. Whilst it may not be possible or even desirable to emulate this in the classroom, the successful infant classroom is a caring environment where the teacher shows interest in all the children and where children are confident in that interest. The children need to know that their efforts are valued when appropriate and they should want to please the teacher. The carer in the home is able to put the child's learning into context, the teacher who has a good, knowledgeable relationship with his/her pupils can also go some way towards doing this.

Opportunity for the child to be the expert

One facet of successful interaction between adult and child is the quality of questioning. Questioning that allows the child to learn that his/her opinions are valued and valid are important in the learning process. For example:

What did you think of that?
Why did you choose that book/style of writing?
Which do you think is best?
What were you thinking of when you wrote that?

Tolerance of error

If the child is to be confident in the interaction that he/she experiences in the classroom, the adult should accept differences in opinion and errors. If incorrect response and deviation from standard opinion is not accepted the child will soon learn who has the power in relation to literacy and could choose to reject all that goes with this. This is important in all attempts that children make in reading and writing and in discussion of these. Indeed, the way a child deals with the error can be enlightening in itself. If a child is given no chance to self-correct he/she may not learn that this is a good strategy to employ and the teacher may not learn whether or not the child has recognised the error for him/herself.

A further issue that could be touched upon here involves the way in which the child is expected to interact with the adult. Both Cox and Kingman stress the importance of acceptance of non-standard dialect in the early stages of learning; this is not to deny children the right to learn Standard English but to prevent young children developing negative attitudes to either non-standard dialect or Standard English. Indeed, Kingman stresses Standard English is the right of all. However, undesirable messages can be given to children about literacy if unrealistic expectations are placed upon them or genuine attempts at expression criticised. Use of Standard English should indeed be developed in all children, but if non-standard dialect is the language of the home it will be a while before the child is able to choose appropriately between standard English and non-standard dialect. In fact, children are not to be assessed on this until Level 7 in oral language and only to begin to use the structures of whether Standard English at Level 4.

The ability to listen

Quality interaction requires time and opportunity. Young children often take some length of time to articulate ideas and opinions, and the temptation in a busy classroom to fill in the words for them is sometimes overwhelming. However, again, for children to develop a sense of what literacy is about and an understanding that it is something that is meaningful to them, they need to have time to put their ideas into words.

Sharing books or his/her own writing with the child provides an excellent opportunity for interaction. However, much criticism has been levelled at teachers in the past for the way in which they do this. Studies describe a dual queueing system in which the teacher 'hears a child read' and 'marks' writing at the same time (Southgate *et al.*, 1981; Bennett *et al.*, 1984). The messages that are passed to the child about the importance of his/her contribution are significantly negative under this system and there can be little or no quality interaction.

Interaction between child and child can be judged to be of a low order and is often not of the nature intended by the teacher. However, where children have the opportunity and where they have a model for interaction they are able to engage in high-level interaction. In classrooms where a conferencing approach is used in writing (i.e. where the child is encouraged to discuss his/her writing with peers and adults, see Graves, 1983 and Calkins, 1983) children have been shown to be able to discuss their writing in a useful way. Also the encouragement of discussion during writing can help children to clarify their ideas about the content of their writing even if they are not yet able to discuss style and form.

Play also provides opportunities for interaction between child and child and, where the teacher has provided the context for use of literacy, interaction can centre around the functions and use of reading and writing in a context that makes sense to the child.

Another aspect of the effective classroom is the quality and amount of feedback given to the children (see Table 1, page 51). Positive response to children's efforts is an important element in successful learning. There should be opportunities for appropriate praise, positive feedback, and acceptance of child opinion and active involvement in literacy activities. Praise is an important factor in motivation, but it must be appropriate praise. Unwarranted praise, as well as too little praise, can have a detrimental effect on motivation. Tizard *et al.* (1988) showed that children tended to overestimate their ability. Whilst positive images are important and success certainly breeds success, successful reading and writing at the infant level has sometimes been equated with getting through the books in the reading programme and neat, tidy writing. This can lead to complacency on the part of high achievers and despair on the part of those children who do not succeed initially on this narrow front. The ILEA *Primary Language Record* (ILEA, 1988b) includes conferences with children about their achievements in literacy and provides the opportunity for positive feedback on a broad front and individualised learning objectives.

Praise should also be focused so that the writer or reader is quite clear about *what* is good. 'A good piece of writing' does not show the child which part of that writing is valued by the reader and can again lead to success in literacy being assessed by the child in terms only of what the teacher mentions – which may only be spelling, neatness and length in writing and correctness or even speed in reading.

Demands made of the children and the response to these demands should be consistent. There is some evidence that teachers stress procedural aims over cognitive ones and sometimes provide feedback that is inappropriate for the demands made (Bennett *et al.*, 1984). It can be revealing to ask the children in class what, in their opinion, makes a good reader/writer; the answers tend to show what the children think is valued by the teacher. This was done as part of the National Writing Project and answers referring to writing included 'having a sharp pencil', 'no spelling mistakes', and 'sitting quietly'!

Bennett *et al.* (1984) also stress the importance of observing the process of the activity and providing feedback to children with reference to the cognitive demands of the task. Discussion with children while they are engaging in literacy activities can both assist their learning and also provide information for further teaching. Feedback given to children under these circumstances is individualised and, if constructive, can help the young learner progress.

Finally, and of great importance, positive feedback which is achieved through the close and informed relationship between teacher and child allows the child to retain a sense of involvement in the activity and a feeling that literacy is relevant and pertinent to him/her.

CONCLUSION

This chapter has considered the role of the teacher as a facilitator. It has shown how teachers have an important role to play in making decisions about the range of resources used and the contexts in which they are employed and that these decisions will affect the way in which the child interprets and understands the task of learning to be literate.

The way in which teachers respond to children was also shown to be of great importance. Interaction was highlighted as being a crucial factor in learning and one that plays a significant part in the effective infant classroom. The response of the teacher to the child can be a major factor in the way that the child interprets the relevance of literacy to his/her life.

6 The teacher as model

Whilst the role of the teacher as facilitator has been placed first in this book and represents an important element of the teacher's role, it should not be seen as the only one. It cannot be considered sufficient to provide a rich environment for the children to develop within. The criticism made by Donaldson (1989) of the 'minimal teaching movement' implies that this first role could be considered by some teachers as the only one. This is far from the case. The way in which the teacher both demonstrates and participates in literacy activities will have a profound effect on the child's learning.

In consideration of the way in which the young child learns in Chapter 2, the comparison was made between learning in the home and learning in the school. The success of learning within the home was shown to be partly due to the way in which the learning took place within a context that made sense to the child. When what was taught could be put within the child's frame of reference, understanding was more easily achieved. For example, when the child shares the writing of a shopping list or telephone list with a parent, or, when reading a story to the child the parent is able to refer to that child's previous experience and relate it to an episode in the book. Thus, the child can see how an adult reader or writer uses literacy and can learn from this.

Children learn the language and emulate the behaviour of the home in the first place and then the language and behaviour of those they admire, be it family, peers or the latest TV craze. For this reason the previous chapter emphasised the importance of providing a wide range of literacy activities in order that children can see the relevance of their literacy learning to their own life and that of their families. It must be recognised that not all families will involve children in the writing of shopping lists and the reading of stories, but children will have learned behaviours and attitudes from observing those of their families. Thus, in the same way, the teacher should be seen to participate in literacy activities both with the children and in their own right as an authentic adult activity. The close relationship that develops between the good infant teacher and the individuals within his/her class in some way mirrors the relationship between child and parent or carer. Thus, the teacher can show children that literacy is not just something that is learned in school but something that is engaged in by adults as part of everyday life.

Research into language learning has highlighted the important role of interaction. Wells' work (1987) showed the extent to which the quality of interaction affected children's language development, and many of the studies of classrooms discussed in Chapter 3 cite a high level of inter-action as being an important feature of the successful classroom (Tizard and Hughes, 1984; Bennett *et al.*, 1984; Mortimore *et al.*, 1988 and Galton and Simon, 1980). Where high quality interaction is to be achieved the implication is that the model of teaching will not, for the most part, be didactic. For the interaction to be of a high quality it should be more like the interaction in the home where the child and adult interact as equal partners, and it is often initiated by the child and takes place within a context that is real to the child. This can only occur when the child is respected as an active learner and when the task makes sense to the child. This has implications for the teaching style adopted; it does not mean that there should be no teaching but that this can be more subtle and better suited to the age of the learners. Where teachers are actively involved working and sometimes learning alongside their pupils they can model the attitudes and behaviours associated with literacy.

Both Bruner (1977) and Vygotsky (1962) emphasise the importance of cooperation in learning. Vygotsky's 'What the child can do in cooperation today he can do alone tomorrow' sets the scene for a classroom situation in which the teacher and children work together, where there are opportu-nities for the child to work with peers, older or younger children, or with the teacher towards shared goals. As will be seen in the following chapter this element of cooperation between peers offers exciting possibilities for effective classroom management. However, it also directs the teacher towards activities which allow children to work with a skilled adult (either the teacher or another adult in the classroom) on literacy activities in which they can learn from the skilled behaviour of the adult.

Bruner also describes the process of 'scaffolding' whereby appropriate social interactional frameworks are provided so that the child can learn as part of contexts and routines that are familiar to him/her. This element of routine is another useful aspect to successful classroom management and will be discussed further in the following chapter. The activities described below, such as story time, register, shared writing sessions and other parts of the individual routines of an infant classroom, offer many opportunities for the teacher to model the reading and writing processes.

The role of the teacher as model, therefore, has two parts. The first to be described is that of participant, where the teacher can be seen to take part in and enjoy literacy events which are a real part of adult life. This allows the child to recognise the relevance of these activities, unlike a child who was in a class of mine who, when hearing that I was going to the library to get some books to read, asked, 'Why? I thought you could read already!' The second aspect to this role is that of the teacher as demonstrator. Here the teacher plans activities which give him/her the opportunity to demonstrate how the experienced reader and writer goes about the task. These 'demonstrations' can be either general opportunities when writing or reading with the children or ones which are targeted to show specific points to particular children or, of course, they can be a mixture of both.

TEACHER AS PARTICIPANT

For children to understand that literacy is something that is valuable in its own right and not a whim of the school system, they need to have the opportunity to see it in use. Some children will come from homes where the literacy events are very similar to those of the school, whereas other children may come from homes where literacy plays a less important part. The classroom that emphasises the role of print in the environment and provides a wide range of literacy events will go some way towards enabling all children to see the relevance of what they are learning, but this can be assisted by the teacher making sure that the children have the opportunity to see him/her reading and writing.

Messages to other teachers, records, and notes home to parents are all regular parts of the teacher's day when he/she needs to write as part of his/her job. But how often are these relegated to playtime or lunchtime? Yet the opportunity to show the children how we write and also the range of purposes for which we write should not be missed. Children are interested to know when the teacher has received a letter or when they have written one and are going to post it. Teachers who write stories for their classes provide two excellent opportunities to show their own use of the writing process. Firstly they can excite the children's interest in the story by situating it in the known environment and even by writing the children themselves into the story. Secondly the teacher, as author, can demonstrate to children the power of the writer over the text, changing, elaborating or otherwise altering the text or storyline.

There are also opportunities for teachers to share the writing tasks of the children. Sitting with a group and attempting to compose at the same time as they are will not only help the teacher to perhaps understand some of the difficulties a young writer might be experiencing, but can also provide opportunities for genuine interaction about the writing process. If the teacher has taken part in a writing activity, he/she can show how writers reflect on their work and analyse it critically. The teacher can also discuss the difficulties he/she may have experienced, how to go about overcoming them, how to decide what to write about, opening strategies, and any other appropriate topic in which the child may show interest.

It is to be hoped that the days are gone in which children might have been heard to say 'Reading? Oh I finished that in Miss Jones' class.' However, it is still important for children to understand that adults do continue to read after leaving school and do so for pleasure. It is certainly the case that not all adults do this which makes it all the more important for the teacher to take every opportunity to show how enjoyable reading can be as children may not see their own families reading for pleasure. A look at the newspaper or a quick visit to the library at lunchtime is not cause for guilt but celebration.

Children will be interested to know that adults have favourite authors and preferred types of books in the same way as they do and that there may be things that they read for different reasons, for example to find information, enlarge knowledge etc. There are plenty of opportunities for reading during the working day – messages, letters from parents, dictionaries, information books, equipment catalogues and many others. As with the opportunities to write these can be taken as a important demonstration of the role of reading in adult life.

Similarly, there can be times when the teacher could read with the children. Southgate *et al.* (1981), when recommending that children should have some time each day in which to read a book of their own choice to themselves, also recommended that the teacher should read a book of his/her choice at the same time. Unfortunately, in busy classrooms, the time is more often used for administrative tasks or reading with individual children. However, there are other schools where the whole school sits down (or lies, kneels, etc.) to read: dinner ladies, secretary, teachers, children. This can give powerful messages to the children about the value and pleasure gained from reading.

A system that expects children to learn to read using only reading schemes does not allow children to learn to exercise choice in their reading. In fact, the child who said that he did not want to read a particular book was regarded as a trouble maker! Yet the ability to choose is a vital element in adult reading and children should be given the opportunity to learn this skill as well as all the others. Teachers can help with this by modelling critical behaviour and exercising choice, for example in giving reasons for their choice of story book, stating their preferences and explaining these.

In the previous chapter the value of providing play environments in which there were opportunities for children to use literacy was discussed. These environments will also provide the teacher with the opening to intervene in the play, and model desirable literacy behaviour. A newspaper or recipe book in the home corner could remain untouched until the teacher intervenes by 'visiting' the home and drawing attention to it.

Literacy 'conferences' with children provide excellent opportunities for the teacher to participate in the literacy activities with the children and to engage in high-level interaction. In discussions about pupils' writing or reading, the child should be allowed to be the expert; this gives the teacher the genuine occasion to interact with the child on an equal basis. At the same time the teacher can demonstrate the sort of attitudes that he/she would hope children would adopt in peer conferencing, as shown in the following example of a conference between the teacher and a six-year-old girl:

Teacher Tell me about your story.
Child A ghost . . .
Teacher There's a ghost in it is there?
Child I'm really asleep but I heard a noise downstairs and I thought it was . . . was a g . . . ghost.
Teacher Have you ever seen a ghost?
Child No (*laughs*), but I saw one on Ghostbusters.
Teacher Oh yes! What are you going to do about the noise in your story?
Child I don't . . . go and have a look and . . . and scare it away.
Teacher Oh, how will you do that?
Child I'll knock all the tins . . . tins in the cupboard . . . you know . . . down and . . . and the ghost'll be scared and disappear.
Teacher That sounds exciting. I like the way you have made the word 'crash' seem loud with those squiggly lines.
Child Yes, I saw that in a . . . in Meg and Mogg.

Thus the teacher can participate in literacy activities, both those that the children undertake in the classroom and by showing how literacy is a part of everyday life to be used and enjoyed. They can also participate by sharing in the child's literacy experience in genuine dialogue with the child. As Frank Smith (1988) said, teachers themselves should be part of the 'literacy club'.

TEACHER AS DEMONSTRATOR

The behaviourist view of teaching reading involves the breaking down of the process into small skills that will be taught separately until the reader eventually puts them all together to make a whole. However, psycholinguistic theory has shown how adults read without following any strict linear pattern and recommends that reading be taught in a holistic way. Critics of these ideas fear that the skills of both reading and writing will not be learned by all children by practice alone. It is here that the modelling of reading behaviour can demonstrate the skills of reading *as part of* the process of reading, the skilled reader showing the learner how they go together to make a whole. Indeed there are often opportunities for the teacher to demonstrate many aspects of literacy in a way that will make sense to the child because they occur in a familiar or real context.

Big books

These, although expensive, offer many potentially rewarding uses, apart from the enjoyment of the story. The format and print is large enough for all children in a class group to see them clearly, therefore each child can see the way the book works. The teacher, just by picking up the book and looking at the title and author, by by-passing the first page to find the text and by following the print down the page and from left to right and turning the pages is demonstrating how books work: the conventions of layout and directionality. In the reading of the book and by comments made, the teacher can demonstrate how the reader anticipates or speculates on what may happen next or refers back to a previous part of the text to monitor understanding.

Storytime

Opportunities to read or tell stories to the class or small groups should be found as often as possible. There are so many valuable purposes to this activity, apart from that of pure enjoyment, that this should be given a priority position during the day when children are fresh and eager to listen and respond. Tizard and Hughes (1984) report that storytime in the nursery school was often relegated to the end of the day when children were tired, or used to fill a gap rather than as a valuable activity in its own right. Storytime provides an ideal arena to demonstrate the attitudes of the experienced reader: enjoyment, criticism, reflection etc. Names of authors and style of books can be discussed with the youngest reception children. Children can be encouraged to reflect on what they enjoyed (or did not enjoy) about a story if the teacher can articulate this for them in the first instance.

Comprehension is a vital aspect of reading, but one that many poor readers find difficult. Not only do they find it hard to understand a story they are reading but also they experience difficulties in monitoring comprehension. Teachers reading a story to the class can demonstrate without spoiling the story being read, the way that they monitor comprehension. They can articulate the metacognitive skills of comprehension by showing how they question or re-read if something seems to not make sense, how they speculate about what may happen next, how they may be able to summarise the main idea of a text and how they use previous knowledge and experience to improve understanding.

Quiet reading time

A time set aside for everyone in the class to read quietly has been suggested as a useful opportunity for teachers to read a book of their own choosing while the children are doing the same. Here teachers can model concentration, enjoyment, involvement and many other aspects of reading that cannot be taught in a lesson.

Real contexts for reading

There are many occasions when adults have to use their reading skills to locate information. Whenever possible it is worthwhile demonstrating these to children, both to show that they do occur as part of adult life and also to show what is involved in the process at the level appropriate to the children. Using a dictionary, finding out a fact, finding the bus times, looking for a phone number and many other opportunities can be taken either for real or in intervention in play.

So the opportunities are manifold for the teacher to model the various uses of reading, the enjoyment and workings of story and positive attitudes to reading. The appropriate strategies and attitudes can be demonstrated in use, whether it be locating information, receiving written communication or enjoying reading for pleasure. The skills can be shown as appropriate, and particularly the importance of monitoring comprehension and the links that hold the text together as this is something that cannot be taught in any structured lesson but has to be learned through experience.

THE TEACHER AS A WRITER

One of the most important ways in which the teacher can model the writing process is by writing in front of and alongside the children. This is encouraged by both the National Writing Project and the National Curriculum. Finding time to sit down and write at the same time as the class can be rewarding in more ways than one. Not only does it demonstrate to the learners that adults do write and can experience the same difficulties as they do, but it can also be revealing for teachers to have that experience (and to rediscover for themselves) the tentative nature of composition.

As with reading there are also opportunities during the school day to show the uses of writing in everyday life: messages to other teachers, letters to parents, order forms, memos etc. Children are often fascinated by the sight of an adult writing, they like to question and to comment on style of handwriting and content. A message board in the classroom can provide a place where written language is displayed by both children and teacher. It can contain reminders, posters of coming attractions, messages, notes between teacher and child and child and child, and many other real uses of writing to be contributed to by all, and read by all.

Similarly, there are occasions when teachers write as part of their work with children and again opportunities arise to model how an adult writes. These can allow teachers to show that they too experience difficulty with writing if the position is awkward, that spellings may need to be checked, that they need to re-read what has been written and may need to change it if it does not 'sound right'.

Shared writing

In addition to incidental opportunities to write, a planned, shared writing session provides an ideal chance to model many of the different strategies used in writing. The teacher sitting at an easel with paper and felt-tip pen can model all the aspects of transcription and composition in a way that uses skills in context and demonstrates attitudes and behaviour. Whether the children are four and five and developing directionality, ideas about the uses of writing and simple notions of sound-symbol correspondence and letter formation, or whether they are seven and thinking of drafting and redrafting ideas, brainstorming, trying out punctuation and different styles and structures, the teacher will model behaviour and can also focus on various learning points as part of the writing activity.

Thus, by writing with and alongside children, teachers can model the strategies and behaviours associated with the process of writing and can demonstrate ways of reflecting, in a conscious way, on the written word.

Links between reading and writing

Thus far, consideration of the role of the teacher as a model has taken reading and writing separately and has considered how these can be demonstrated to children. The teacher, as a writer or as a reader, can also model to children the links which exist between writing and reading, and can show how the whole process of literacy is an integrated one, and that the two elements do not exist in isolation.

The rewarding nature of an activity such as writing stories for children has already been mentioned. This can also demonstrate very effectively for children the way the writer has power over the written word and how the writer must make considerations about the audience. Teachers who write stories to read or tell to their classes can involve the children in the reworking of that story. They can show how endings can be changed, new characters written in and plots elaborated. This will give young readers/writers insights into the creation of written language which will help to develop their concept of literacy.

Story-telling is another way in which the nature of literacy can be shown. The very action of telling a story to children obviously extends their experience of story as a genre, but also the teller uses different words on different occasions, elaborates or condenses plot or descriptions and responds in an immediate way to the audience. This mirrors the thought processes of the writer when revising text and provides learners with models of behaviour that could be adopted in their own writing.

The letter or message is also a powerful medium for providing young writers with an immediate (or not too delayed) response to their writing. Hall (1987) describes an occasion when the teacher took the opportunity to draft and redraft a reply to a message from the headteacher and the valuable discussion that ensued. Whilst children should, of course, be given the chance to write their own messages and letters, the teacher, in a structured shared writing session or as an impromptu activity to respond to a real need, can show how the reader must be in the mind of the writer during composition and how the reader may respond to the writer.

Metalinguistic awareness

This was discussed in Chapter 2 and, although there is no clear agreement as to how metalinguistic awareness relates to reading or writing ability, there is evidence that the two are connected, although the relationship is not necessarily causal. The early reader or writer is not able to articulate more than the most simple aspects of this but this does not mean that he/she cannot subconsciously utilise knowledge gained from the experience of using language. Thus, the teacher who is able to reflect upon language in a way that is accessible to children could help children to develop this important aspect of literacy development. All the examples given as to how the teacher can model the process of reading or writing have allowed children the opportunity to observe the ways in which the reader or writer exercises choice and control over the language he/she uses.

In a more basic way the teacher can also introduce to children the first elements of metalinguistic language while writing in front of them or by using a resource such as the teacher's stand from the *Breakthrough to Literacy* materials. In this way they can use terms such as word, line, letter etc. which are basic to any discussion about the written word but which, until learned, can cause confusion in the learner. Also demonstrated can be the way in which words can be interchanged, added or omitted by the writer, again demonstrating the control that the writer exercises over language.

CONCLUSION

This chapter has considered the role of the teacher as model. It has shown how this is a powerful instrument in assisting young children's learning, given the way they learn through imitation and interaction. The teacher has been shown to model the literacy process in two ways. Firstly by participating in literacy activities to show children how this is a valued and useful part of adult life and not merely something to be learned and then forgotten, and secondly by observing an experienced reader or writer employing these skills, the young learner can observe how the various component skills of literacy mesh together to make a coherent whole.

7 The teacher as manager

Chapter 5 considered the teacher as facilitator, where the type of classroom environment that might produce a rich environment for learning literacy was discussed. However, it is not enough to place children within a stimulating and supportive situation. This is the criticism levelled by Donaldson (1989) in her criticism of the 'minimal teaching movement' in which a stimulating environment is considered to be sufficient. The teacher has also to manage that situation and the other learning tasks that are provided within it. Teaching infants has been variously described as juggling plates in the air or having a farmyard of chickens pecking at your legs! Indeed there are times when it can seem like that. For this reason effective management is an essential part of any classroom for the sake of both learners and teachers alike.

Research studies undertaken in primary classrooms over the past ten years have given some indications of the type of learning conditions that may assist children's progress. Similarly, research into children's learning and the increase in our understanding of the process of literacy has also enlarged our knowledge of the way in which children learn. Much can be gained from these studies and there are indications of ways in which the teacher's task can be made more effective without becoming more onerous. However, many of these ideas do ask a great deal of the teacher who has a class of more than thirty demanding youngsters.

Galton and Simon (1980); Bennett et al. (1984); Tizard and Hughes (1984) and Mortimore et al. (1988) all point to high levels of interaction being beneficial in the classroom. They discuss elements such as the opportunity for extended conversation with individuals and higher order questioning as being important aspects, although Mortimore et al. suggest that too much interaction with individuals in the junior classroom, at least, can be counter-productive. To this can be added the research perspectives of Wells (1981) and Bruner (1965) as well as many other writers who emphasise the important role played by interaction in children's learning, and most particularly in their learning of language. Earlier chapters have considered the ways in which enhanced interaction between children and adults can assist children's progress. However, all of this takes time. Time to spend with individuals and small groups, time to listen, time to allow the child to formulate and express his/her thoughts. This is why it is suggested that too much interaction with individuals can be counter-productive, because it could leave time for little else and only reach a few children at occasional intervals. As with everything else it is a part of the whole picture, not the whole picture itself.

Good assessment and record keeping is singled out by Bennett (1984 and 1989); ILEA (1988) and Mortimore et al. (1988). Also, of course, this is an aspect emphasised by, and now a legal requirement of, the National Curriculum. However, the type of records and assessment that are advocated are not the traditional kind of record that records what has been done or assessment procedures that give a reading age from a group or individual word reading test; they are those that record children's literacy behaviour and serve a diagnostic function. Ways of going about these will be discussed in Chapter 8, but these kinds of record keeping and assessment, while undoubtedly worthwhile, are most certainly time-consuming.

The importance of feedback being given to children, along with praise and a positive attitude is also stressed (Galton and Simon, 1980; ILEA, 1988 and Mortimore et al. 1988). While praise certainly takes no more time than censure, appropriate feedback, like interaction, is time-consuming. Similarly, the advantage of providing children with activities that are relevant and purposeful and which they clearly understand is highlighted by Bennett et al. (1984); ILEA (1988) and Tizard et al. (1988). It could be seen to be much less demanding of teacher time to give out worksheets and quick instructions, but this is less beneficial to learning and, as will be discussed later, does not really save time in the long run.

If these aspects of research make demands upon teacher time, fortunately there are also factors that can assist the teacher and enable him/her to use the learning situation to its full potential. Many of the studies (Tizard et al., 1988; ILEA, 1988; Mortimore et al. 1988 and Bennett and Kell, 1989) recommend cooperative learning. Bennett recommends that teachers of four-year-olds adopt Bruner and Harste's advice (1987) and consider children as 'social beings' rather than 'lone scientists', which is what often happens in current practice. This also reflects much of Bruner's work where he argues for children learning alongside other children or adults.

Many studies consider different aspects of classroom management, which will be discussed in greater detail later in this chapter. Emphasis is placed on routine, match and task design as being important factors of effective classroom management.

The active involvement of the children in what they are asked to do and the importance of tasks that are embedded in context rather than for their own sake are seen to be elements of a well-run classroom. This backs up the argument propounded by Donaldson (1978) in which she discusses how it is the 'disembeddedness' of some learning situations that cause children problems.

To this is added the climate of the classroom and the range of activities covered. An atmosphere in which children are allowed to make errors and to find solutions within a framework is put forward as a successful learning environment. This also, by giving children more autonomy, can free the teacher of some of the endless questions that can be so time-consuming if he/she is the sole decision maker in the room. A range of language activities and approaches to teaching are seen to be important by Bennett et al. (1984); ILEA (1988) and Tizard et al. (1988). This encourages the teacher towards a flexible approach to organisation and should give children opportunities to work both alongside and away from the teacher.

Tizard et al. (1988); ILEA (1988) and Mortimore et al. (1988) all stress the importance of establishing good relationships with parents. Particularly where this is more than just a PTA (Mortimore et al.) and where the links were on a more personal basis with the class teacher (ILEA). Many studies have shown that parental involvement in the teaching of reading has a great impact. However, there is still some question as to whether this will have the long-term effect that it appears to have had in the short-term. Certainly Tizard et al. (1988) did not find that parental involvement in reading aided learning in the schools they studied, contrary to the results of the Horringey study (Tizard et al., 1982).

Each of the elements considered above offer potential, not only for developing more effective learning for young literacy users, but also for managing the classroom situation in a more efficient and effective way.

COOPERATION AND COLLABORATION

Both Bruner and Vygotsky emphasise the importance of learning together. The cooperative nature of learning is something that can be overlooked in a classroom where emphasis is placed on competing to achieve the right answer. Even in an infant room where children talk happily and productively at play, there is sometimes a feeling that maths and English should be conducted quietly and individually. When collaborative discussion is not encouraged, the talk has been shown to be of a fairly low order in language tasks (Bennett *et al.*, 1984). Similarly, Galton and Simon (1980) highlighted the anomaly that, while primary children did work in groups, they rarely worked as a group.

Bennett and Kell (1989) recommend that teachers should employ less individualisation since effective individualisation is impossible in classes of the size of the normal infant class. Plowden (1967), whilst admiring the principle of individualisation, suggested that only seven or eight minutes a day would be available to each child if all teaching were on an individual basis. This view has been reinforced by HMI reports since. Added to this Tizard *et al.* (1988) reported that children found reading a frustrating activity with no one to help with unfamiliar words. There are many opportunities in language learning for children to work collaboratively and cooperatively, either amongst themselves, with older peers or with adults. Not only do these provide children with worthwhile learning contexts but also, because they avoid the notion of the teacher as the only arbiter, pass some of the responsibility over to the children which releases the teacher to work with other children.

There have been many projects in which children have been given the chance to read or write with other children. This obviously has benefits for both sides of the partnership. There are as many paired reading schemes as there are schools using them. Yet the basic condition of the teacher providing a scenario where children and adults, or older children, read together occurs in many schools or, more usually, in the home. The practice of the teacher being the only person to interact with a child about a book is long gone, and releases the teacher from the onerous task of hearing every child read every day, a practice that has given rise to much criticism of the resulting lack of attention paid by the teacher to the child while they are reading. In some schools children from classes higher up the school come to read with infant children (or older infants with younger). Here the older child has the responsibility for choosing an appropriate book with the younger child and reading it with him/her. In other schools use is made of secondary school children or adults from the community to spend time sharing books with children. This does not mean that the teacher never reads with individual children but it does mean that the time when spent is of a high quality and not snatched at odd moments or break times.

Similar projects have been tried with writing activities. The use of an adult or older child as a scribe for young children to enable them 'to compose at greater length than they can manage to write down by themselves,' part of the National Curriculum Programmes of study, (DES, 1990) is a long-standing one. Also there are opportunities for children to work collaboratively to produce a piece of writing. This gives rise to all sorts of worthwhile discussion about the decisions a writer must make during composition and editing. This is particularly useful when it takes place at the word processor; the appearance of writing on the screen adds an objectivity that enables the writer to see the text in fine copy early on in the process and assists judgement. Also the very nature of the word processor encourages revision; moving and deleting text is part of the process and can free young writers from the stigma attached to error. Even very young children can experience writing on a word processor, either through devices such as the concept key board or by working collaboratively with a more experienced peer.

Group work, where children can work together on a project, or syndicate work, where they have different tasks and work towards a shared goal, provides good opportunities for interaction about the process as well as the product and, since the children themselves have responsibility for the activity, releases the teacher to work with other groups or individuals. For example, reception children could work as a group to prepare the home corner for Goldilocks to find after the three bears had gone for their walk, or Year Two children could work as a syndicate to find out from a range of sources information about a topic of mutual interest to produce their own reference book.

Classrooms which encourage an ethos of caring for each other and sharing offer scope for children to help each other. This can be with words or comprehension in reading or, in writing, with spelling, remembering items and providing a friendly but critical audience. Peer conferencing, as a part of a conferencing approach to writing, can give even the youngest children the experience of having peers comment upon their attempts and to reflect themselves upon the attempts of others. The procedure described by Calkins (1983) can be adapted and used even in the reception class. The class, in a 'group conference' can listen to another child's composition being read, repeat what they have heard, with practice ask questions about it and even say which parts they liked in a group conference. Once children have experienced this when led by the teacher, they have an agenda from which to work with other individuals when the teacher is not beside them. Peer tutoring in reading has been in existence for many years, the most common form being when older children share books with younger ones, and has been found to have benefits for both parties. Also, when members of the same class work together sharing a text the mutual support provided gives added reading time for the children and a sharing of experience and expertise.

ACTIVE INVOLVEMENT OF THE CHILDREN

The importance of the child being an active participant in the learning process has been stressed by researchers into learning and by studies of classroom practice (Galton and Simon, 1980; Bennett *et al.*, 1984; Tizard and Hughes 1984 and Mortimore *et al.* 1988). A classroom in which the children are engaged on tasks that make sense to them and that are embedded in context is one in which the teacher has opportunities to engage in appropriate cognitive interventions and to interact with individual children. In a similar way, in the classroom where children are allowed to make mistakes and encouraged to find solutions to problems for themselves, the teacher is not required to be the provider of all answers and all information. Thus there is less necessity to answer procedural questions and 'police' the activity.

All infant teachers will recognise the different efforts required of them in the following situations. In the first, children are asked to follow instructions to cut out and then sequence a series of pictures, to stick them on to another piece of paper (to be collected from the teacher when required) in the 'correct' order and to write a neat and correctly spelt sentence under each. In the second, children are working independently on the first draft of various writing activities to do with Christmas, such as a shopping list, a letter to Father Christmas etc.

Analysis of the first activity identifies four aspects which will ensure that the teacher is constantly in demand to respond to children's needs.

1   The task has no real purpose other than that the teacher asked children to do it. There appears to be no meaningful context outside that of the activity as prescribed.
2   There is only one solution to the activity, therefore many children will be unwilling to take risks in their sequencing and the teacher will also need to check each finished product. Arguably an activity such as this would provide more learning opportunities if children were encouraged to choose their own sequence and then justify it.
3   Writing is expected to be neat and correct at the first attempt, ensuring that the teacher will be occupied in providing spellings and robbing the children of the opportunity for tentativeness that an experienced writer needs.
4   Resources are in the gift of the teacher, again ensuring that he/she has plenty to do.

In contrast, the second example provides children with a context that makes sense to them, they are encouraged to be tentative and error is tolerated. In this instance the teacher will have more time to interact with children about the task while they are doing it and to make appropriate interventions in the learning process.

Play is another learning context which is of great value to the young child. At play children can set their own goals and explore literacy in a way that makes sense to them. Bennett and Kell (1989) found that teachers often undervalued play, either relegating it to the end of the day or when 'work' was finished, or making little effort to structure it or to intervene in the process. By planning a variety of literacy contexts for play, the teacher is providing a valuable arena for learning. Also, because play is self-motivating, children will need less supervision than for some other activities. That is not to say that the play should be ignored, but that the planning and preparation can be done at intervals to vary and structure the provision, and regular intervention can be a planned part of the teacher's schedule.

Chapter 5 looked at the kind of classroom environment that provides a wide range of literacy activities for children to explore. This implies that children will be reading and writing on their own, with peers and with adults undertaking a range of literacy tasks. Thus, the teaching of reading is not left to hearing children read every day, indeed the emphasis is on *quality* time spent sharing books with children rather than the regulatory two pages while the teacher is doing umpteen other things. Tizard *et al.* (1988) found that children spent more time reading in classes where there were opportunities for paired and shared reading (up to twenty-seven minutes per child per day) rather than in classes where the teacher spent a great deal of his/her time hearing children read.

So, the classroom where the children are actively involved in literacy events that are embedded in real contexts, where some tentativeness and risk-taking is encouraged and where learning is shared and cooperative is a place where children will learn. However, in addition, the teacher who encourages autonomous learners, avoids inhibiting expectations and provides a wide range of literacy activities, will find that he/she has to spend less time controlling and regulating the classroom.

MANAGEMENT STRATEGIES

Good management is essential to an efficient learning environment. This includes the way the activities are presented to the children, how well those activities have been designed and matched to ability, and how they are monitored.

Presentation

The way that activities are presented to children will affect not only how valuable they are as a means of learning but, often, how much teacher input they require. When children are unclear about what they should be doing, when they do not have the appropriate resources to hand and when the task has a tightly prescribed outcome, they have to constantly ask the teacher about the next step. Monitoring the questions that children ask is a good way of gaining information about how successful your management is.

Young children respond well to routine. In a well-run classroom the workings of the day are predictable, many instructions do not have to be given because they have been the same since the beginning of term. Children who read quietly together for a certain time each day know the procedure and the rules. They will not have to have repeated instructions as they would if they were sometimes required to read in silence, sometimes on chairs, sometimes without choice, etc. Thus a pattern of activities and a predictable procedure give security to young learners and render the learning more effective.

Bennett and Kell (1989) report how teachers of four-year-olds often stressed procedural rather than cognitive aims. For example, in a task that required a child to sequence some pictures the teacher emphasised the colouring and cutting rather than the sequencing itself, even though she herself was clear about the cognitive aims. They also report that teachers often failed to give enough information about what the child was to do or a sufficiently detailed explanation. Again the more prescribed the outcome required, the more detailed the explanation has to be.

The availability of resources is also a key feature of a well-managed classroom. Where the area is rich in print, with a wide range of texts, reference books, words used in context, writing materials, etc., and where the child is encouraged to use these, he/she can take more responsibility for his/her own learning. It seems that, if children can be confident to make their own decisions and choices within a framework, the resulting learning will mean more to them. Also, where the children are allowed some autonomy, the teacher does not have to spend so much time making their decisions for them.

Task design

The emphasis of this book has been on literacy learning taking place in real contexts and with the active involvement of the children as literacy users and decision makers. This implies that task design will not consist of merely choosing the right worksheet or page from a workbook. It involves providing an environment where literacy is evident in its range of forms, providing a variety of activities where children can use literacy for real purposes, providing a balance of teacher-directed and self-initiated tasks, good match and appropriate cognitive interventions. This also implies that the skills and processes of literacy will be used for exploring other curriculum areas; recording, expanding, explaining and finding out, for example. This in itself, apart from providing a context for literacy learning, enables the teacher to use his/her time more effectively.

Bennett *et al.* (1988); ILEA (1988) and Tizard *et al.* (1988) all report the desirability of allowing a range of activities and approaches. Bennett *et al.* (1984) found that the most successful teachers in particular areas of language were not those who practised those particular skills a great deal, but those who provided a broad range of language activities. For this reason free choice should not always be the only writing or reading task; whilst children certainly do need the opportunity to choose, they also need agendas to choose from. If they have opportunities to see/hear the teacher reading and writing (in storytime or a shared writing situation) from a range of literacy uses and styles, and if they are encouraged to try a particular use or style on occasion, they will have the experience and confidence to choose for themselves on other occasions.

The National Curriculum stresses the importance of building on the young child's experience of literacy in the outside world, and of using it in a range of real contexts (DES 1990: Programmes of Study 6, 7 and 13–15). The use of a variety of audiences other than the teacher, apart from being a valuable learning experience, again releases the teacher from being the sole arbiter and frees him/her to spend time on monitoring children's progress and appropriate cognitive interventions. Where children understand the relevance of the task to hand, either because they have chosen it for themselves or because it has a purpose that they understand and value, not only will the learning be more lasting, but many of the time-wasting procedural questions will be avoided.

Tasks designed to practise particular skills are often ineffectual for young children because of their disembeddedness. Children may not learn to use the skill as they are unable to transfer the exercise to a real context when they meet it. Comprehension exercises often provide examples of poor task design; questions can be answered without any understanding of the meaning of the text. For example, try the following:

The praggle weevled pottly down the sprood. It hadged then jorred and off it weevled again without its kniff this time.

1   How did the praggle weevle?
2   What did it leave behind?

To answer these questions does require an understanding of language itself and how it works, but it does not need any understanding of the text. Much more effective ways to monitor comprehension would be through discussion, drama, art, writing in role and other more relevant and effective means.

Chapter 5 described a learning environment where there was ample opportunity for children to explore reading and writing in a number of different ways. The self-initiated nature of these activities render them also self-maintaining. Where there is a balance of self-initiated and teacher-directed activities underway in a room, the teacher has more time to spend with those children who are working on teacher-directed tasks. This does not mean that the teacher will never intervene in play or similar activities, but that there is choice, as opposed to constant attempts to keep up with the bare necessities.

In a similar way, in a classroom where the tasks are often open-ended and the children are encouraged to make decisions for themselves, there is less need for the teacher to spend much of the time checking and correcting. For example, although a worksheet with a precise recognition and colouring task seems an easy option, if there is only one right way decided by the teacher, the child must constantly seek reassurance, whereas a collecting, sorting, or drawing task can exercise the same skills but allow more freedom to the child.

This all requires careful monitoring. It is not enough to set children on to activities; children's response and behaviour during the process is both informative about the learning process (see Chapter 8) and informative about how effective the presentation and match has been.

Match

Much has been written about the importance of matching task to ability. HMI documents have focused on the importance of avoiding the dangers of overestimation or underestimation. Bennett *et al.* (1984) report that teachers appeared to focus their task design on the middle band of ability in the classroom. The consequence of this was that high achievers did a large percentage of practice, whereas low achievers had more new knowledge to contend with, instead of the other way round, which would be more appropriate. The solution to this is not to prescribe a language scheme for children to follow doggedly, but constantly to observe and monitor children's progress and to provide the sort of range of activities and literate environment that have already been discussed. Fortunately for the English teacher the use of literacy in real contexts is something that can be tackled by the child at his/her own level. The design of a poster to advertise a coming event can be a challenge to children within a wide range of ability. However, in the same way as the teacher acknowledges and builds on the child's previous experience when the child starts school, language activities should build on previous experience to provide a sequenced and structured programme. Thus, within the activity described above, the teacher will intervene with individuals or groups at a level appropriate to them. Equally it would be important that, for example, a particular aspect of language such as poetry would not be something that is mentioned once or twice and that children are expected to be able to write *some time*. Poetry would be read, discussed, explored through art and drama and written in shared writing sessions before the child was expected to produce an individual poem of their own.

In Chapter 2 the contribution that Vygotsky has made to our understanding of learning was discussed, particularly the zone of proximal development. This is the area between the child's present developmental level and his/her potential level and is discovered by setting the child a problem that is just beyond their grasp and allowing them to solve it with an adult. From this can be discerned what the child is capable of achieving at the present and what the child will be able to achieve soon. More will be written about assessment of children in the next chapter, but it seems important that the teacher knows the child's level of achievement in order to ensure that the tasks that the child is undertaking are of a level within which learning can occur.

The problem of underestimation has been one that played a major part in the teaching of reading and writing. The notion that reading and writing are difficult and that young children starting school know little or nothing about them is not one endorsed by the National Curriculum. Children are seen to be capable of having a go at reading and writing from the beginning, provided they are not expected to get it all right the first time and that the context is one that makes sense to them. A teacher working as part of the National Writing Project in Dorset told me of her work with a class of nine-year-olds in which she asked them to write stories for her top infant class. The junior children enjoyed the activity immensely and would come to the teacher's classroom at spare moments to finish off their books. The top infants not only enjoyed reading the books but also wanted to undertake a similar project themselves for the reception class. This they did with a large measure of success and a great deal of learning.

Bennett *et al.* (1984) report that although word puzzles were used in some schools it was mostly the high- and mid-attainers that were expected to do them, although there is no reason why low-attainers should not gain as much or more from such activity.

Overestimation would appear to be less of a problem in broad-based literacy activities because of the way the learner can use literacy at their own level across a range of tasks. Overestimation is a problem, though, when the class are expected to follow a programme of workbooks or cards which follow a scheme preordained by a publisher rather then the teacher who can focus tasks on individual children. It can be that pages of workbooks that are intended to develop a particular skill or concept are rendered meaningless to the learner because of the disembeddedness of the task and the prescriptive nature of the requirements.

Thus it seems that management of the learning environment is an important factor in ensuring that children learn effectively at the level that is appropriate to them. However, it is also an important factor in enabling the teacher to have the time necessary to provide the monitoring and interaction that is so necessary in the learning of young children.

LINKS WITH THE HOME

Examination of how children learn in the home has given us insights into how school learning may be made more effective for young children. Certainly when the aims and expectations of home and school coincide, learning is more likely to take place. Tizard *et al.* (1988); ILEA (1988) and Mortimore *et al.* (1988) all found that teachers and schools where there was more parental involvement were more successful, although this seemed to depend on the nature of the links, in that the traditional PTA that could often be dominated by a minority of parents was less effective than personal links forged by individual classroom teachers. It is not the place in this book to discuss the success or otherwise of the many and various parental involvement projects that have been tried. It is the task of the teacher to ensure that links are forged with parents so that aims and expectations can be shared. Many educational controversies have been fueled by lack of understanding, and time taken to explain and collaborate with parents is well spent.

When the teacher's requirements as to correctness of writing or what is to be done with a reading book that is brought home have changed, it is important that the parents are consulted or the child will be caught in the middle of a conflict of expectations. A reading record or diary to accompany the book that is taken home can help avoid misunderstandings. This can signal to parents what expectations the teacher may have of their child with this book, for example:

a   Your child will not be able to read this book but will enjoy hearing you read it to him/her.
b   Your child knows some of the words in this book and will be able to join in reading it with you.
c   Your child can read this book to you.

A space left for parents to comment is also useful since it encourages them to enter into dialogue with the teacher about their child.

Many parents are willing to come into classrooms and work alongside their own children and/or others. This, apart from adding that extra pair of hands, has the benefit of developing the partnership between school and home and allowing the child to see the value placed by the parent on the activities undertaken in school. However, it is not only parents who can be useful visitors to the school; grandparents, brothers, sisters and other family members may have more time to visit than parents. Also, other members of the community can help forge links between school learning and the outside world and can provide different models of language, dialect or accent.

Extra adults or older children can usefully join in with paired or shared reading, can act as scribe for children to write at greater length than their mechanical skill would allow, act as editorial consultant for young writers, and write or read in different community languages as appropriate. The enhancement of learning and developing partnership with parents makes the practice valuable in its own right, but no teacher with thirty plus infants will deny the benefit of more adults in the classroom to work with the children.

CONCLUSION

Thus it can be seen that, although the role of the teacher of literacy at Key Stage One is an onerous one, if teachers follow advice given by researchers into children's learning and the National Curriculum, there are many aspects to the way children learn and the way teachers manage the classroom situation that can render this task more effective and less daunting. This chapter has considered the importance of cooperative and collaborative learning and the active involvement of the children in what they are doing. It has been stressed that some expectations on the part of teachers can reduce effectiveness and cause their task to become more difficult. The management strategies of presentation, task design and match were discussed and practices that research studies have found to be helpful or harmful were considered. Finally the valuable role that parents and other members of the community can play was stressed.

8 The teacher as assessor

The previous chapters which have described the role of the teacher have considered a person who provides a stimulating literacy environment, takes an active part in the literacy process him/herself, models this to the children, and manages the learning situation effectively. However, these roles on their own cannot work effectively unless the teacher is also able to observe and monitor and progress of children. Assessment is a part of the teacher's job that has gained public prominence in recent years, although all good teachers have continually assessed children in an informal way all the time. Almost every decision made in the class about an individual child is based on assessment of some form.

It is not the intention here to discuss the assessment procedures for the National Curriculum, but to consider assessment in more general terms. In the first instance the types and purpose of assessment will be discussed and then these will be related to young children learning literacy. Finally three children will be considered, both in relation to the attainment targets for English and also in terms of classroom strategies.

There are three purposes for assessment: summative, formative and diagnostic. These do not need to be exclusive categories, indeed, it can be argued that the most useful assessment fulfils each of these purposes. *Summative* assessment sums up the teaching that has been done and produces a final picture of the success of a teaching programme. *Formative* assessment is on-going assessment which affects the decisions that are made while the learning programme is in effect. *Diagnostic* assessment diagnoses the child's strengths and weaknesses and provides information about further teaching points.

In addition, forms of assessment can be related to their sources of information and designed as: *norm-referenced*, where the child is judged in relation to a formerly determined 'norm', or *criterion-referenced*, where the child's performance is assessed against previously determined criteria.

There is also the informal type of assessment which teachers undertake as part of their daily practice in the classroom. This does not follow any formal procedure but is an integral part of the teacher's role. It can, of course, be very subjective but is nonetheless a useful tool to build up a picture of the child and an effective one when used by experienced teachers in conjunction with more structured forms.

For the purposes of this book it is intended to consider formative and diagnostic assessment as these are the most useful to teachers in their daily work. It is also intended to discuss both informal and more structured assessment.

The importance of effective diagnosis and record keeping was stressed in many of the studies examined in Chapter 3. Good assessment is fundamental to many aspects of good practice. In order to match work successfully to children it is necessary to be able to assess them. Vygotsky (1978) describes the zone of proximal development as being the area between where the child is now and the child's potential level at that time. It is within this area that successful learning can take place and, thus, the teacher should be able to ascertain this in order to target the child's teaching appropriately.

Young children thrive when they feel secure in the situation in which they find themselves. Asking children to do something that they do not understand or that is too difficult for them is a way of undermining any sense of security. However, children do also enjoy a challenge and will learn from such. Indeed boredom and/or frustration are two frequent causes of disruption by children in the classroom. Everyone has experienced the satisfying feeling of having planned an activity that has been enjoyed by the children and that has taken them forward in their learning. For this to happen more often than purely by chance, the teacher has to know his/her children well and plan accordingly.

Chapter 7 considered the effect of expectation upon children's learning and emphasised how important it is to have high expectations. Our expectations are based upon our judgement of children's ability and the more information we can use to arrive at this the more accurate these will be. The importance of stressing cognitive outcomes in learning activities was also considered. In our interaction with individual learners if they are well known to us in their strengths, weaknesses and previous experience, we will be better able to target the focus of that interaction in such a way as to advance their understanding.

The form assessment takes is based on views about the nature of what is being assessed. Many widely used reading tests stem from the belief that reading is a series of skills that need to be taught separately and then welded together by the reader. These tests tend to test these skills as separate entities, for example the word recognition test that assesses children's ability to recognise words out of context. Other tests have attempted to assess other skills such as comprehension, but these are all on decontextualised tasks which younger children in particular find difficult. These tests give information about how the child performed in relation to his/her peers on a similar test, but do not give diagnostic information. Most teachers do not need to be told that a certain child is performing below average at reading, they have already come to that conclusion. Teachers will often mistrust information from tests that does not match their own perception. For example, if a child who was reading quite well in the classroom was found to have a below-average reading age, this result would be put down to test conditions rather than misjudgement on the part of the teacher. This is not to say that norm-referenced tests do not serve some purpose; teachers like to know how their group of learners compare to a national norm, especially in small schools where there is little opportunity for comparison. However, for the classroom teacher, assessment that gives indications for further teaching is more useful and effective.

Formal assessment of writing at the infant stage is not widespread and informal assessment has tended to centre on correctness and conventionality. This is linked to ideas about learning to write such as were discussed earlier.

If we consider what the teacher actually needs to know in order to plan his/her teaching we can get a better picture of what forms of assessment are useful. Firstly, it is necessary to know *where the child is* that is what the child already knows and what background experience the child is bringing to the task of learning literacy. Secondly, we need to know *where the child is going*, in other words we must have a clear picture of what constitutes progress in literacy and be sure to focus our assessment on to this. Thirdly, the teacher must have ideas about *how the child can be helped to progress*. Good assessment should be clearly linked to what the next step might be in order for it to be of real help to the teacher.

WHERE THE CHILD IS NOW

Chapter 2 considered how children come to school already having some knowledge about the form and processes of literacy and that it is important to build upon this. We can build on the knowledge children already have provided that we take time to notice what this might be. Traditional views about the role of the teacher presupposed that the learning programme would take place despite of the child not because of him/her. For example, all children starting school would be given the same pre-reading book or activity and expected to copy or trace over the teacher's writing.

Where there is provision for children to read and to write from the beginning and the teacher spends time in observing how children go about this, a picture can be built up about what the child can already do. Figures 1 and 2 show two four-year-olds' attempts at making a shopping list. They had both assisted the teacher in a shared writing session and Colin had copied the teacher's list.

At first glance it might seem that Colin is a better writer than the child in figure 1. Indeed, according to some criteria he could be judged as such. However, when we consider that the list was copied, there is very little that we can actually tell about what Colin knows about writing. He has good hand-eye coordination to be able to copy, but close inspection of his letter formation shows that this has been a difficult and painstaking task.

Figure 1 shows a child who has understood the purpose of a list as a means of recording, even if he does not know about layout. He understands that symbols can be used to record meaning, whether these are pictures or letters, and he knows that these join together to make words. He knows what the letters of the English language look like, although he does not understand sound-symbol correspondence. He has good spatial awareness and fine motor control.

Figure 1

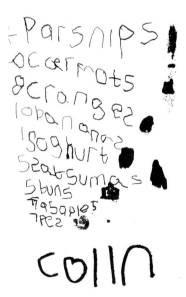

Figure 2

In reading, children's progress used to be judged by their rate of progress through the reading scheme. Reading records tended to consist of a list of the books read. These gave some indication of the pace at which the child moved through the scheme, but did not tell the teacher how the child had read these books, nor did they give any indication for further action. However, recent advances in the types of records kept result in the teacher observing and recording children's reading behaviour rather than merely what they have read. Value is given to the way children show an interest in and understanding of literacy. Thus, the child is observed on starting school as to what interest they show in books, how much they know about the way a book works and whether they can recognise any words or letters in the environment.

WHERE THE CHILD IS GOING

The attainment targets for the National Curriculum provide a much broader range of goals than success on one reading test or progress through a scheme. In both reading and writing, increased awareness of what the processes of literacy entail has enabled teachers to judge children on more than how near they are to correctness. Not only is their existing knowledge considered, but also progress can be monitored according to a wide range of abilities.

The learning of early writing involves the mastery of certain skills such as hand-eye coordination, motor control and visual memory. It also requires certain knowledge about conventions of directionality, linguistic structures, sound-symbol correspondence and letter formation. An understanding of the concept of writing, attitudes to it, originality, design and voice are also important factors. Children will not move forward at an even pace on all these fronts, and indeed will be starting from different points when they come into school. The teacher who understands the writing process can assess children's ability in all these areas and judge when it may be appropriate to intervene to move the child forward in one or more of them.

Similarly in reading, attitudes, cueing strategies, comprehension, book skills, search for meaning and understanding of the concept are all parts of the process. In addition there are the skills of auditory and visual memory, knowledge about sound-symbol correspondence and the conventions of written language to be learned. The teacher who understands how these are used and knows how much the child already knows can help that child to develop further strategies and skills when appropriate.

HOW THE CHILD CAN BE HELPED TO PROGRESS

The most important purpose of assessment for the class teacher is to provide indications of where and how to proceed. Where reading schemes and series of workbooks are relied upon to provide the structure for the learning programme the teacher feels secure in what they are doing. However, as has been shown, practising literacy on primarily decontextualised tasks which follow the agenda of a publisher rather than the child's individual performance cannot really be assured to bring the child to his/her potential.

Observation is the prime tool in assessment at this age. This can be either general observation of the child at work or at play or structured observation such as miscue analysis (Goodman, 1967). It is important to observe the child at both teacher-directed activities and at self-initiated ones. The child at play can set his/her own goals and choose from all his/her knowledge and experience to achieve these goals. Thus, observation of the child at play can provide insights and even surprises that might not be gained from observation of a prescribed task. However, a prescribed task can provide the opportunity for the teacher to observe a particular behaviour, for example, letter formation in the copying of a caption for a mother's day card.

Structured observation would include miscue analysis and running records as described in the *Primary Language Record* (ILEA, 1988b), observation of the child in a variety of contexts, analysis of samples of writing and interviews with the child and with the child's parent(s). Information gained from these observations can be fed back into the other aspects of the teacher's role. For example, the child who is observed to be using primarily picture cues in their reading can see the teacher demonstrate the use of context or semantic cues when reading a big book with a small group. Similarly, the child who does not appear to understand the concept of written language can be helped by the introduction of a letter-box or message-board in the classroom.

In order to examine how assessment might work, including the National Curriculum levels of attainment, three children, who were judged by their teachers to be at about Levels 1, 2 and 3, have been observed in a general and structured way. It is intended to consider what these observations tell us about what each child already knows, what they need to learn and to give suggestions as to how they might be helped to progress. The children all come from the same large primary school. They come from mixed social backgrounds, although they are all children whose mother tongue is English. For the purposes of this discussion they have been chosen as children who are making progress at literacy learning. The intention is to give a picture of a child at each level of Key Stage One and to consider ways of assessing these children.

CLAIRE

Claire is aged six years and two months and coming to the end of her time in the Year One class. She is a quiet and thoughtful child who gets along well with adults and children but does not have a special friend. She particularly enjoys maths.

General assessment

Claire appears to enjoy reading, she will often choose to look at a book in spare moments. This is usually one she knows well and she will spend some time on one book. Although there is a writing corner in the classroom Claire does not use it.

13.7.90
First thing in the morning the children come in and choose something to read. Claire has brought in the colouring she has done from some templates at home which she waits to show the teacher. Later she picks up a book that she has often read before and reads quietly. She does not share it with any other children or talk about what she is reading. She appears interested and to be following the words of the text.

During the morning she plays in the home corner. This is set up as a kitchen/home area and has many opportunities for literacy play: newspapers, recipe books, instruction booklets, message board etc. Claire takes the role of mother, she goes shopping then cooks the dinner. She uses a recipe book and follows the instructions carefully.

When set on the task of writing about the Sports' Day that they had had the day before she is slow to gather her things and to settle on to task. She takes time to sharpen her pencil and fusses about which crayons to use. She draws her picture first which is detailed and neatly coloured. The writing itself shows a personal response to the Sports Day, correct directionality, good line and word concepts, some knowledge of initial sounds and use of a full stop.

Literacy conference – 16.7.90

Claire speaks quietly and fluently although she sometimes cannot be heard. She is pleased to talk about her writing but says she does not enjoy it very much. Children in this class have two writing books. In one they write stories, reports, poems etc., and in the other they do 'planning'. This is a development from Highscope (1979) in which children write what they intend to do when they play. It has the dual function of focusing their attention on their intentions in play and provides an opportunity to practise writing a sentence.

Claire can talk about the writing she has done although she cannot read it back word for word. She says she prefers writing in her planning book because 'I can keep looking back . . . most times I copy out pages . . . every time I've got one right I copy that.' Her favourite piece of 'writing' is a page of sums.

She says that she enjoys reading and names two or three books that she enjoys: '*The Tree House* and there's one called *There's a Dark Dark House.*' She reads *Not Now Bernard* by David McKee with enjoyment, putting in expression and is very concerned for it to make sense (see running record). She finds it more difficult to talk about the story. When asked what she thought might happen when Bernard's mother went to wake him in the morning, she said, 'She'll have another baby then she'd have more children.' She had obviously understood the literal meaning of the text but was unable to predict what might happen next in the context of the spirit of the story.

Running record

```
Extract from NOT NOW BERNARD by David McKee

"Hello, Dad", said Bernard. Bernard's Dad
"Not now, Bernard", said his father.

"Hello, Mum", said Bernard. Bernard's mother
"Not now, Bernard", said his mother.
Mum                         outside      he's
  "There's a monster in the garden and it's going to eat

me", said Bernard.          Bernard's mother
"Not now, Bernard", said his mother.
                            Outside
Bernard went into the garden.
and said
      "Hello, monster", he said to the monster.
'Roar' said       and        little
  The monster ate Bernard up, every bit.
And then he
Then the monster went indoors.

"ROAR", went the monster behind Bernard's mother.

"Not now, Bernard", said Bernard's mother.

The monster bit Bernard's father.
"Ow"
  "Not now, Bernard", said Bernard's father.
                  on the table in front of the television
  "Your dinner's ready", said Bernard's mother.
(pause)          it
She put the dinner in front of the television.
He
The monster ate the dinner.

Then it watched television.
                              /(mumbled)
Then it read one of Bernard's comics.
  Then
And broke one of his toys.
                      given
  "Go to bed. I've taken up your milk", called Bernard's mother.
"I'm a monster" said the monster
The monster went upstairs.
(pause) "But I'm a monster", said the monster.

"Not now, Bernard", said Bernard's mother.
```

uses pictures

Claire read confidently and with expression. She followed the words when she got them right but had to pause if her memory of the story got ahead of the words themselves. Where she did not follow the words accurately her interpretations made sense and followed the storyline and language of the story. Her embellishments show good understanding of the story

(*Bernard's father said 'Ow' when bitten on the leg*) and use of book language (*Roar said the monster and ate Bernard every little bit*). When she did get ahead of herself in the story she was able to find where she was by recognition of the words.

Writing samples analysis

Claire has directionality and the concept of a word well established. Her motor control is good and she produces letters of similar size and with mostly correct orientation. She understands that writing should carry a message and can read some of her writing back. She could not read the story of the three bears but knew that there were only two bears in the picture because 'The other's with mummy in the kitchen making a cake.' She appears to have some words that she can write correctly, although these may be copied as she suggests in her comment in the literacy conference. She can write her friends' names correctly, these have probably been copied off the trays showing that she knows to how to find words she cannot write herself. She knows about the initial sounds of words. Her personal writing shows originality and is individual to her.

National Curriculum

With reference to Claire's performance in relation to the National Curriculum levels of attainment she appears to satisfy all conditions at Level 1. She certainly recognises that print carries meaning and can recognise individual words or letters in familiar contexts. She is interested in reading and can talk in simple terms about the content of stories. Although she is working towards Level 2 she has not really achieved any of the statements as yet.

In Attainment Target 3 she is certainly at Level 1. She does use pictures, symbols or isolated letters, words or phrases to communicate meaning. Her attempts at conventional spelling do show understanding of the difference between drawing and writing, she shows some knowledge of letter shapes in response to sounds and uses groups of letters to recognise words. In her handwriting she does form letters with some control over size, shape and orientation. However, as with the reading, there is very little of Level 2 in her writing.

It has already been pointed out that there is a large gap between a child at Level 1 and one at Level 2. Claire has a good grounding at Level 1 but has some way to go before she will achieve the standard of the statements at Level 2.

Strategies for development

Claire is making good progress in her reading. She enjoys books and is beginning to talk about what she has read. She can recognise some words and is definitely reading for meaning. As she gains more experience and confidence her range of strategies will be extended and she will be able to express more informed opinions about what she has read.

For her teacher it would seem important to build up Claire's confidence as a writer. She is concerned about correctness and this seems to stifle her creative ability and enthusiasm to write. She should be encouraged to use the writing table where her efforts need not be 'judged' by the teacher. A character in the classroom, such as a teddy bear, for the children to write to and who will write back to them could be a useful device to help Claire see some of the purposes of writing. She should also be able to see the teacher composing and making errors so that she understands that errors are a natural part of the process of composition. Progress on other fronts would seem to be dependent on Claire developing her confidence and writing more fluently. As her reading develops her sight vocabulary will grow. Her existing knowledge of initial letter sounds could be built through games like I–Spy and her store of words that she can spell confidently will be increased through practice in various types of writing. Too much emphasis at this stage on individual skills could take away the little confidence she has in writing and the fact she has already developed some strategies for herself means that the teacher can feel confident to let her develop for herself for a while.

EMMA

Emma is aged seven years and nine months and is coming to the end of her time in the Year Two class. She is a cheerful and outgoing child who has many friends. She enjoys language and is particularly good at PE.

General assessment

Emma enjoys reading and writing and is confident in both. She will often share a book with a friend in her spare moments and spends a lot of time in the writing area making her own books and writing poems and stories.

5.7.90

When the children come in in the morning Emma picks out the book she was reading yesterday and continues to read it with a friend. They take it in turns to read aloud to each other, occasionally stopping to chat about other things.

During the morning she has the opportunity to work at the writing table, here she starts to make a book 'The Song and Poem Book about Animals Becoming Extinct'. She gets as far as the outside cover with title, author's name and a dedication on the first page.

Later she dictates to a parent on the word processor the caption for some work the class did earlier in the week 'To trick the seagulls you could put plastic food on top of the real food and put it in a plastic bucket.'

Literacy conference – 6.7.90

Emma is pleased to talk about her literacy experiences, particularly the books she has made. She shows a good understanding of the purpose and structure of books and particularly enjoys writing stories. She can talk about the writing she has done, is able to read it back and often remembers how she felt while writing it: 'This one was hard, I didn't know how to end it.'

Emma chooses a book to share carefully, looking through a few before selecting *Maggie and the Monster* by Elizabeth Winthrop and Tomie de Paola. She has read this before and can read it word-for-word correctly, although she reads carefully and slowly. The story is about a child who finds a baby monster in her bedroom, she helps the monster find its mother who lives in the broom cupboard. Emma interprets the story on the literal level, she says she enjoys the book because it makes her laugh and reminds her of her little brother.

When questioned about books that she enjoys she mentions stories and poems. When questioned further about using books to find out about things she is less confident:

Teacher   What do you do if you want to find out about things?
Emma   Ask the teacher.
Teacher   Do you ever look in books?
Emma   I use a dictionary.
Teacher   Suppose you wanted to find out more about the owls we had in earlier in the week?
Emma   I'd ask the teacher.

Miscue analysis

Emma reads a poem she has not heard before from *Please Mrs Butler* by Alan Ahlberg. She reads slowly and carefully with some attempt to follow the rhythm of the poem and make sense of it. When she comes to a word she does not know she uses some phonic skill, as in 'cossy' for cosy, or the overall conformation of the word, as in 'whenever' for whether and 'earth' for death. This seems to be in preference to context even to the extent of using a non-word like 'cossy'. Although, when she completely lost her way in the last line, she stopped rather than say something she knew was wrong. She had, however, understood the poem and could talk about it in relation to her own feelings about playtime.

COMPLAINT

The teachers all sit in the staffroom.

The teachers all drink tea.

The teachers all /smoke cigarettes

As /cosy as can be.   [cossy written above /cosy]

We have to go out at playtime   [got written above, have underlined]

Unless we bring a note

Or it's tipping down with rain

Or we haven't got a coat

We have to go out at playtime

Whether we like it or not.   [whenever written above]

And freeze to death if it's freezing   [it is written above]

And boil to death if it's hot.   [earth written above]

The teachers can sitin the staffroom

And have a cosy chat   [we inserted]

We have to go out at playtime;

Where's the fairness /in that ?   [T when the fair written above]

Writing sample analysis

Emma's writing shows enthusiasm for what she is writing and a concern to get it as she wants it. She uses the rubber a great deal, often erasing a whole picture before starting again. She is also beginning to look back at what she has written to put in words that have been left out and to change spellings. She is not yet revising the content. She is certainly developing her own voice in writing, and this is particularly evident in the owl writing (opposite) where her enjoyment of the visit shows through. She is also developing an awareness of audience in the explanations she gives. She demonstrates a knowledge of many features of writing such as the exclamation mark and apostrophe although she does not use them correctly yet.

Monday 18th June 1990

whne the balloon took me up and up and up

onn day I was takeing the Dog for a wallk
whne I Sore an old man Selling bollon's
I was Lucky Becaose I had £2 the bollon's whre
£2 and I went over and got a balloon
I went on my whay agin and
thene the horrible thing haponed the
thene ba loon start ed taking me up and up and
up and thene the bolln burst and
thene I fell dawn in a crater
and thene the Dog wnet made and
he wnet woth woth and til
we got back woth and Erthe and
thene I fell dawn to my bed whte
a bump and thene out of wake up.

what a brilliant story!

Monday 9th July 1990

this morning Amber's mummy
came to school to show us some
Barn owls and a towny owl and were
they brot Raydar in He was suting
on a soart of thing whitsh had
two wooden bits at the botom and
a bent metal bare in the middle
and Mrs Pusey saide its hod
Pote therefits hands up whne the owl
did a wewe. and the male has a white
Chest and the Female has a speckled
and taye both are chest
barn owls.

well done call a
What do we
lot of birds eggs?
clutch

Her spelling (below) shows a good grasp of sound-symbol correspondence and she is starting to develop a store of words that she can spell correctly. Her word book shows that her attempts at spelling are less good when she is really unsure of how to spell the word, however she still uses most of the obvious sounds in her attempts.

Bb		Cc	
brow		CoCSSkar	Cox's Cave
Barx		Cod	could
Barry		Cilod	coloured
Bothday	birthday	CowtSh	coach
Bethlehem		ColiShe	College

R r	S s	
Room	Sa es	space
Rafacchn reflection	Sab	
Rojer	Sowr	Saw
	Sam	Some
	SuLLqTas	Stalagmites
	saLLgmas	Stalagtites
	Sex	See
	Saw	
	ScoTLond	
	Satdrday	
	Story	

Her handwriting (above) shows good control over the size and shape of letters and she forms most of her letters in a way that will make them easy to join up when she starts to do this.

National Curriculum

Emma was selected as a child who would be about at Level 2. She can read some straightforward signs and labels but is less confident when they are new. She cannot recite the alphabet but uses a word book competently. She can use all the cues in reading but appears to rely too heavily on phonic cues to the detriment of meaning. She is well able to talk about the stories she has heard or read and can predict what will happen next. She is not fully fluent when reading aloud even with texts she knows well, but clearly understands and enjoys her reading.

In writing she has not yet developed an understanding of how to break her work into sentences. However, the structure of her writing is both coherent and sequenced showing an understanding of openings and endings and the need to take the reader's understanding into account when writing. She produces recognisable spellings of many common words: whne, sore, bollons, brot etc., and she also knows many simply monosyllabic words: dog, he, was, did etc. She is beginning to recognise that spelling has patterns and applies this knowledge in some of her attempts to spell: sore(saw), soart(sort). She also knows the names of the letters of the alphabet. Her handwriting, although fair for a child of her age, is perhaps not quite at Level 2, she does still mix upper and lower case letters on occasions. Her ascenders and descenders are evident but not always clearly above or below the line of writing.

Strategies for development

Emma is making progress in her reading and writing. She appears confident in both and chooses to use them when she can. For her teacher it would be important to maintain this while extending her experience and skills.

She could be encouraged in her book-making, which she enjoys. This, together with her search for improvement as evidenced by the constant rubbing and crossing out, would provide a good starting point for revision and redrafting. She could be encouraged to rework a rough draft before forming it into a book, and as part of this be introduced to sentences. This could first of all be demonstrated by the teacher in a shared writing session and then suggested to Emma in her revision if she does not take it on for herself. Reworking text would also give her the opportunity to go over her work and pick out those spellings that do not look right and to check them with a dictionary.

In her reading she needs to be encouraged in the use of context cues. However, her reading is not very confident and she has not achieved fluency with texts she does not know. It is important not to lose the confidence she does have so intervention would need to be sensitively handled. It is possible that reading books that have predictable repeated patterns of sentences would be helpful to her to develop both prediction and fluency. More discussion of what she reads and of her own writing would help her to start to see meanings beyond the literal.

She seems to be very unsure about the value of print as a source of finding information. This would be an indication for the teacher to examine his/her own practice to discover whether this is something that is peculiar to Emma or whether he/she should raise the profile of the range of uses for reading in the classroom.

ANDREW

Andrew is aged seven years and three months and is coming to the end of his time in the Year Two class. He is an intelligent boy who gets on well with the other children but has no one particular friend. Owing to his father's employment he has moved around a great deal; this is his third school but this does not seem to have impaired his progress. In fact he can talk sensibly about the different demands placed upon him in literacy learning by his different teachers. He responds well to all tasks set, but his favourite activity is drawing which he is good at.

General assessments

Andrew is an avid reader across the whole range, from Roald Dahl through to Enid Blyton, to comics and a variety of information books. He is a competent writer but the standard of his work varies according to his interest in the subject. He will write factual or non-chronological writing from choice. He does not enjoy making up stories and usually prefers to write one he knows.

26.6.90

First thing is the morning Andrew sits quietly and reads *Charlie and the Chocolate Factory* by Roald Dahl. He is absorbed in his reading.

During the morning he is working on some observational drawing of a child with a football. He does not take up the suggestion that he write a caption to go with his picture.

When writing he goes back to continue his work on the story of *The Good Samaritan*. He tries to find a book with the story in but seems confused by a book with that title which has many bible stories in it. He does not find *The Good Smaritan* without help.

Literacy conference – 27.6.90

Andrew is articulate and thoughtful about his literacy experiences. He describes himself as a good reader who can read 'nearly anything at all'. At the moment he is reading through Enid Blyton and talks about her life as well as about her books. He enjoys reading information books as well, saying he looks through them concentrating particularly on the pictures to pick out pieces to read.

He says that he does not enjoy writing as much as reading but enjoys the drawing that goes with it. When he picks out a piece of writing that he likes, he chooses a page where he has copied out the first verse of *The Owl and the Pussycat*. When asked why, he talks about the picture. He is able to articulate what he does when he writes:

> *Teacher* What do you do when you write?
> *Andrew* I think then I write a bit then I think ... it's difficult to explain. I don't know what I'm going to write – how much. I think it's going to be a page and it turns out to be only that much (*indicating a piece of five lines*).

Teacher Do you go back and read it again?
Andrew No, not really.

He describes himself as 'quite good at spelling'. When asked how he managed with the spelling of rhinoceros he said, 'I just wrote it. I wrote it first but I had to rub it out – that (*indicating the 'c'*) was a "k" for some reason.'

Miscue analysis

Andrew reads from a book he has not seen before – *Where the Forest Meets the Sea* by Jeannie Baker. This book has only a small amount of text but this interacts with fascinating illustrations. Although Andrew does not make many miscues, the way he goes through the text is interesting. He takes great care to make sense and also to be accurate as when he starts to read 'push' but changes it to 'hold'. The repetitions he makes are apparently a means of checking for meaning. It is a measure of a good reader that they are able to monitor comprehension and to self-correct. He is also able to use phonic cues (cockatoos). The asterisks in the text indicate where he stopped and talked about the text and illustrations. The reference to the crocodile at the end refers back to the beginning where there was the 'ghost' of a crocodile illustrated at that place. He understands the way the illustrations operate on two levels, the literal and imaginary and his comments during reading mostly refer to this.

My father knows a place we can only reach by boat.

Not many people go there, and you have to know the way through the reef. "I don't know what that is"

When we arrive, cockatoos rise from the forest in a squawking cloud. My "He's imagining"

father says there has been a forest here for over a hundred million years

My father says there used to be crocodiles here, and kangaroos that lived

in trees. Maybe there still are.

I follow a creek into the rain forest.

I pretend it is a hundred million years ago.

On the bank of the creek, the vines and creepers try to hold me back. Cpu

I push through. Now the forest is easy to walk in.

I sit very still. .....and watch. ......and listen.

```
I wonder how long it takes the trees to grow to the top of the forest!
                                                     abargibal
I find an ancient tree! It is hollow.  Perhaps aboriginal forest children

played here, too.
                          It is
I climb inside the tree.  It's dark, but the twisted roots make windows.

This is a good place to hide.

It is time to go and find my father.  I think I hear the sea.  I walk towards

the sound.

My father has made a fire and is cooking the fish he caught.

I like the fish cooked this way.  But then I feel sad because the day has

gone so quickly.  My father says we'll come here again someday.  'I wonder where
                                                                 the crocodile has gone'
But will the forest still be here when we come back?
```

Writing sample analysis

The examples of Andrew's writing are mostly printed because the way his writing is presented makes it difficult to reproduce clearly. Illustrations often run over the writing and the text is not well spaced. The quality of what he writes varies according to his feelings. The account of the visit does not show the vigour, humour, structure, even knowledge of punctuation of the other pieces. It can be seen in these pieces that Andrew knows a great deal about writing, he is aware of his audience, can structure his composition and is developing a style of his own.

Example 1

Wednesday 27th June

If we're not careful there will be no barn owls, elephants, blue whales, tigers, rhinoceros and sparrow hawks. Just because people want them for coats, eggs and things like that. Hunters and poachers are killing elephants because they want there ivory to make ornaments. I don't know why they do it because nobody buys them! They do exactly the same with rhinoceroses for there hornes, Tigers and leopards, like the indian tiger and the cloudy leopard are becomeing extinct because we want the coats, but I think the coat looked better on the animal!

Example 2

<u>Monday 9th July</u>

Barn owls fly so silently that you can't even hear them. The female has got speckles down its front and the male hasn't. The barn owl is the only owl that isn't camouflage. They have brilliant eyes. Tawny and eagle owls look like tree trunks so they can't be seen by other animals. A group of eggs is called a clutch.

Example 3

Friday 6th July 1990

On tuesday we went too woodbury common with Trevor Bartlett and he showed us a badger called stormy and a hedgehog and then we saw some fox alive and then we got back on the coach and then we went to the the coach common and we saw some peat and some sundew that eat flies. and we saw some bog cotton and bog as pidalland some rethelek moss. And then we went too the river otter and we saw a heron and kingfisher that we went too a bird hide and we had lunch. After a lapwing and many other birds.

It was really interesting wasn't it? yes I want to be Trevor Bartlet when i grow

← What a beautiful heron

His spelling is very good for his age, being able to spell both common words and the more difficult ones. Attempts from his word book, where children try the spellings themselves before asking the teacher or using a dictionary, show that he uses phonic cues and some analogy (as in transmittor) if his visual memory does not help him to know the correct version: blizerd, beatyful, cerment, cathidral, transmittor.

Bb

Bulldozer
blizerd
because
beatyful   beautiful

Cc

cerment
cathidral   Cathedral
close
clothes

Tt

tarmdotar
thunder
trobletwit
transmittor
Tusks
tigers

Uu

Andrew's handwriting is legible but poorly spaced. The neatness and accuracy found in his drawings seems to make his handwriting slow to produce and ease for the reader is not considered. His punctuation is good. He uses full stops and commas mostly correctly and knows about apostrophes, exclamation marks and question marks.

National Curriculum

Andrew is a good example of the way a child is not likely to be at any one level across all the attainment targets. Although he is working at Level 3 there are certain aspects in which he is below or even above this.

His reading is fluent even on unknown texts. He reads silently and with concentration, listens to and remembers stories and will talk about them with enthusiasm. He is also beginning to appreciate meanings beyond the literal and has some understanding of the way stories are structured. He enjoys looking at reference books and finds information from them, although he does not use these in a very mature way.

In his writing he can use complete sentences with capital letters but is not yet using a range of connectives, opting for 'and' or short sentences. Although this particular sample does not show it, he can produce a range of models of writing although the standard varies according to his commitment to the subject. His does not like to redraft his work, preferring to finish it at one go.

He fulfils all the requirements for Level 3 spelling. He can spell simply polysyllabic words correctly, uses his knowledge of patterns of spelling and word families to spell and will check through his spellings.

Although some children in the class do use cursive writing and they are all encouraged to, Andrew does not. Purists might also argue that he does not yet have clear ascenders and descenders, although the other requirement of Level 2 are met.

Strategies for development

Andrew is clearly an intelligent child from an educated home background. Criticism of infant classes have been made that these high achievers are insufficiently challenged in their language work. It would be easy to feel satisfied with the standard of Andrew's work and to concentrate on other children. However, this is hardly fair to Andrew and, in fact, such a child would need very little further input to allow him to work on his own for sustained periods and he would enjoy and learn from the challenge.

Many of the teaching points could be covered by capitalising on his interest in information texts and love of illustration. He needs to be shown how to use an index and list of contents and to be encouraged to revise and redraft his writing. At this point it should be mentioned that not all writers revise and redraft their work but children should be shown how to do this so that they can choose whether to or not as they mature as writers. Making his own reference book on a subject that interests him would allow him to research the style and format of these, plan how he would do it, possibly produce a first draft and then produce a finished book on quality paper, possibly word-processed.

There are several small points that could be pointed out from his writing. He is confident as a speller and this confidence would not be jeopardised by helping him to sort out the spelling of 'their/there' and 'too/to'; words that sometimes provide adult writers with difficulty but which should be easy for Andrew to learn before habits become established. He knows about the use of capital leters in people's names but could also learn the other uses. Rather than direct instruction on these points he could be asked to look through books to find examples and work out rules for himself. If he does this, the learning is much more likely to become established than if it is passively received.

Lessons in letter formation of both individual letters and strings of letters will be important at this stage as he moves into using cursive writing. In the first place he will practise this when he is not trying to compose; copying a favourite poem for a class book or in the production of a final draft. The presentation of his writing should be improved as he learns to redraft, and writing for an audience, other than the teacher who is obviously sympathetic, could help. Also encouraging children to have friends read through their writing would cause him to understand the need to take legibility into account.

His reading ability is obviously of a high standard. While it would not be desirable, or even possible, to forbid him to read Enid Blyton, he should be introduced to a wide range of challenging authors at storytime and in his personal reading at school to give him a range of choice.

Thus it has been shown that assessment can cover a broad front and also provide specific information about individual children. It can show where the child is in both strengths and weaknesses and it can give indications as to where to go next both for the individual child and for teachers themselves.

RECORD KEEPING

For a picture to be built up of how a child is progressing, records need to be kept of the assessements as they are made. Many books have been written on the subject and it is not within the scope of this book to look at this in detail. However, some basic principles can be laid down for the keeping of literacy records.

1   The audience must be considered. What records are for the teacher only and which are for a wider audience, next teacher, parents etc.? They should be appropriate for the audience intended.

2   Records should be of manageable proportions. Some records that are suggested are of excellent quality but if they were to be repeated across all the subject areas, filling them in would leave no time for anything else. They should be concise but provide sufficient information in an accessible form.

3   They should record literacy behaviour as well as work done. Providing a list of books read does not give information that can be used in subsequent teaching.

4   They should provide information that is not wholly subjective. However, records that provide only objective information are often so mechanistic as to be time-consuming and uninformative. For example, a checklist of fifty phonic skills does not provide information about how the child uses those skills and in which contexts. A balance between objective and subjective recording should be attempted.

5   The child and his/her parents should be involved in some part of the process. It is important that, even with young children, they should be allowed to share responsibility for their learning. Parents have responsibility for their children for a far larger proportion of the week than the teacher and the information that they can provide is crucial. Also the development of partnership that this encourages has wider benefits than the development of good records.

6   Records should include examples of children's work: pieces of writing, photographs of them using literacy skills at work and at play, and their thoughts about books read. Children themselves should be allowed to choose at least some of the material to be included in this.

CONCLUSION

Assessment and record keeping go together, but not all the information gathered in assessment need be recorded. Some of it would be acted upon immediately, some kept by the teacher as a record over the year and only a selection of this passed on to the next teacher.

Although the type of information discussed here is more time-consuming to collect and record than results of a standardised test, it will provide far more information. It will provide a picture of the child as a learner and literacy user which will be of use both to the current teacher and to those who will teach the child in the future. Effective assessment is the foundation of all other facets of the teacher's role. These cannot be used effectively without detailed, appropriate knowledge of the learner.

Conclusion

'Mrs Fisher'
'Miss'
'Mum'
Even 'Dad'

All these titles which may be used by the child in addressing the teacher show how the young child views the teacher. From the stereotyped, impersonal 'Miss', through the conventional use of the name which is both personal and polite, to the ones which show confusion with the carer in the home. Indeed, the teacher can embody parts of all these roles in the mind of the child.

For teachers themselves the role is also problematic. It has been shown that some theoretical standpoints and even public reports have not helped teachers feel confident in their role. Much is written in books and in the press about what the role should be. Advice is given by politicians, educationalists, parents and the 'man in the street'. The teacher can be left unsure and confused, knowing what he/she wishes to achieve but, very often, without clear ideas on how to achieve this. However, conflicting influences from theory, experience and media hype militate against the quiet confidence with which the teacher should be able to carry out his/her work. With advice and criticism from all sides, the teacher must make sense of the roles of teacher, instructor, child minder, social worker, enabler and many others.

This book has attempted to reconsider the ways in which teachers approach the task of enabling young children to start on the road to literacy. It has considered what being literate actually means and how the emphasis should be on the whole process of appropriate and enjoyable *use* of reading and writing, if we aspire to educating literate adults. The word 'use' is italicised to indicate the importance of enabling children to see literacy as something that has relevance to them and to their whole lives – not just that part of those lives that takes place in school.

Children have played a central part in this book; children as active and interested participants in the learning process. They have been shown to learn best alongside others, both adult and child, and when the learning activities undertaken make sense to them.

Studies of research that provide insights into factors that make teachers effective have also been considered. These give indications for teachers as to which practices assist learning and which may be counterproductive. These practices have been considered under the four roles of *facilitator, model, manager* and *assessor.*

- Facilitator, who provides an environment within which the child can learn.
- Model, who demonstrates the uses and conventions of literacy.
- Manager who manages the learning environment in such a way as to enable each child to achieve his/her potential through appropriate and structured activities.
- Assessor, who observes the process and product of each individual's contribution in order to use the other three roles in such a way as to provide an effective learning programme.

These roles run parallel to the multiplicity of roles suggested in this book. An attempt has been made to examine views about literacy learning and to reconcile changing attitudes to learning with the role of the teacher. The role is a complex one combining knowledge and experience that the teacher has, subconscious feelings about the responsibilities and position of teachers and views imposed on the teacher by external forces who may have a different set of expectations.

This book has gathered together ideas about the task of learning to be literate, with special reference to the National Curriculum; about the conditions under which children may learn; and the experience gained by observers and researchers in classrooms. It takes one particular view of literacy and examines the roles the teacher can adopt to foster literacy development in the young child.

Bibliography

ADAMS, M. J. (1990) *Beginning to Read: Thinking and learning about print.* London: MIT Press.

ALEXANDER, R. (1988) Garden or Jungle? Teacher development and informal primary education, in BLYTH, A. *Informal Primary Education Today.* Lewes, East Sussex: Falmer Press.

APU (1988) *Assessment of Reading: Pupils Aged 11 and 15* (T. Gorman and A. Kispal). London: NFER–Nelson.

APU (1991 in press) *Assessment of Reading: Pupils Aged 11 and 15.* London: NFER-Nelson.

BARR, R. C. (1972) The influence of instructional conditions on word recognition errors. *Reading Research Quarterly*, 7, 509–29.

BEARDSLEY, L. V. and MARECEK-ZEMAN, M. (1987) Making Connections: Facilitating Literacy in Young Children. *Childhood Education*, 63, 3, 159–66, February.

BENNETT, N. (1976) *Teaching Styles and Pupil Progress.* London: Open Books.

BENNETT, N., DESFORGES, C., COCKBURN, A. and WILKINSON, B. (1984) *The Quality of Pupil Learning Experiences.* London: Lawrence Erlbaum Associates.

BENNETT, N. and KELL, J. (1989) *A Good Start? Four-year-olds in infant schools.* Oxford: Basil Blackwell.

BEREITER, C. and SCARADAMALIA, M. (1985) Children's Difficulties in Learning to Compose, in WELLS, G. and NICHOLLS, J. *Language and Learning: An Interactional Perspective.* Lewes, Sussex: Falmer Press.

BRADLEY, L. (1987) *Categorising Sounds, early intervention and learning to read: a follow-up study.* Paper presented to British Psychological Society, London Conference, December.

BRADLEY, L. and BRYANT, P. (1983) Categorising sounds and learning to read – a causal connection. *Nature*, 301, 419–21.

BRIDGE, M. (1989) Learning to Read: A study undertaken by the Leicestershire Literacy Support Service 1986–7, in HUNTER-CARSCH M. (ed.) *The Art of Reading.* Oxford: Basil Blackwell.

BRUCE T. (1987) *Early Childhood Education*. London: Hodder and Stoughton.

BRUNER, J.S. (1965) The Growth of Mind. *American Psychologist*, 20, 1007–17.

BRUNER, J.S. (1977) Early social interaction and language development, in H. R. SCHAFFER (ed.) *Studies in Mother Child Interaction*. London: Academic Press.

BRUNER, J. (1983) *Child's Talk: Learning to Use Language*. Oxford: Oxford University Press.

BRUNER, J. S. and HARSTE J. C. (eds.) (1987) *Making Sense*. London: Methuen.

BRYANT, P.E., BRADLEY, L., MACLEAN, M. and CROSSLAND, J. (1989) Nursery Rhymes, phonological skills and reading: Humpty Dumpty revisited, in *Journal of Child Language* 16, 2, 407–28.

CALKINS, L. (1983) *Lessons from a Child*. London: Heinemann.

CAZDEN, C. (1983) Adult assistance to language development: Scaffolds, models and direct instruction, in PARKER, R. P. and DAVIS, F. A. (eds) *Developing Literacy*. Delaware: International Reading Association.

CHALL, J. (1983) *Learning to Read: The Great Debate* (updated edition). New York: McGraw Hill.

CLARK, M. M. (1976) *Young Fluent Readers*. London: Heinemann Educational Books.

CLAY, M. (1972) *The Early Detection of Reading Difficulties*. London: Heinemann.

CLAY, M. (1975) *What did I Write?* London: Heinemann Educational Books.

CLAY, M. (1979) *Reading: The Patterning of Complex Behaviour*. London: Heinemann Educational Books.

CZIERNIEWSKA, P. (1988) The National Writing Project: thoughts about the early years, in HUNTER-CARSCH, M. *The Art of Reading*. Oxford: Basil Blackwell.

DEFFENBAUGH, S. A. (1976) *The Gifted Reader: Instructional Practices in Connecticut*. Hartford: Connecticut Association for Reading Research.

DES (1975) *A Language for Life* (The Bullock Report). London: HMSO.

DES (1978) *Primary Education in England*. London: HMSO.

DES (1982a) *Education 5 to 9: an illustrative survey of 80 first schools in England*. London: HMSO.

DES (1982b) *The New Teacher in School: A Report by HM Inspectorate*. London: HMSO.

DES (1987) *National Curriculum: Task Group on Assessment and Testing: A Report*. London: HMSO.

DES (1988a) *Report of the Committee of Inquiry into the Teaching of English Language* (The Kingman Report). London: HMSO.

DES (1989a) *English for ages 5 to 16* (The Cox Report). London: HMSO.

DES (1989b) *Reading Policy and Practice at Ages 5–14: A report by HM Inspectorate.* London: HMSO.

DES (1989c) *English in the National Curriculum* (Key Stage One). London: HMSO.

DES (1990) *The Teaching and Learning of Reading in Primary Schools.* London: HMSO.

DONALDSON, M. (1978) *Children's Minds.* London: Fontana Books.

DONALDSON, M. (1989) *Sense and Sensibility – some thoughts on the teaching of literacy.* Occasional Paper No. 3. Reading and Language Information Centre – University of Reading.

DURKIN, A. (1988) *A Classroom Observation Study of Reading Instruction in Kindergarton.* Technical Report No. 422.

EDER, D. (1982) The Impact of Management and Turn Allocation Activities on Student Performance. *Discourse Processes,* 5, 2, 147–59.

FISHER, R. (1989) Bibliophiles in the Making, in *English In Education,* 23, 1, 8–13.

FRANCIS, H. (1982) *Learning to Read. Literate behaviour and orthographic knowledge.* London: George Allen and Unwin.

GALTON, M. and SIMON, B. (1980) *Progress and Performance in the Primary Classroom.* London: Routledge and Kegan Paul.

GARNER, R. (1987) *Metacognition and Reading Comprehension.* Norwood, N. J.: Ablex.

GARTON, A and PRATT, C. (1989) *Learning to be Literate: the development of spoken and written language.* Oxford: Basil Blackwell.

GOODMAN, K.S. (1967) A Linguistic Study of Cues and Miscues in English, *Elementary English,* 42, 639–43.

GOODMAN, K. (1982) *Language and Literacy I & II* London: Routledge & Regan Paul.

GRAVES, D. (1983) *Writing: Teachers and Children at Work.* Exeter, New Hampshire: Heinemann.

GRAY, J. (1980) Article in *Times Educational Supplement,* 7 November, p. 17.

GUTHRIE, J. T. (1973) Reading comprehension and syntactic responses in good and poor readers, *Journal of Educational Psychology,* 65, 294–9.

HALL, L. (1987) Come Back Teacher, *Times Educational Supplement,* 16 October, p. 24.

HALL, N. (1987) *The Emergence of Literacy.* London: Hodder and Stoughton.

HEATH, S. (1982) What no bedtime story means: narrative skills at home and school, in MERCER, N. (ed.) *Language and Literacy from an Educational Perspective*, vol. 2. Milton Keynes: Open University Press.

HOFFMAN, S. and KNIPPING, N. (1988) Spelling Revisited: The Child's Way. *Childhood Education* 64, 3, 284–7.

HOHMANN, M, BANET, B., and WHELKART, D.P. (1979) *Young children in Action.* Ypsilanti, Michigan: Highscope Press.

ILEA (1988a) *The Hackney Literacy Study.* London: ILEA Research and Statistics Branch (pp. 12, 20, 63, 111, 142, 143, 144, 154).

ILEA (1988b) *The Primary Language Record.* London: Centre for Language in Primary Education. (pp. 123, 171).

JULEIBO, M. (1985) The literacy world of five young children, *Reading Canada Lecture*, 3, 2, 126–36.

KLEIN, A. and SCHICKEDANZ, J. (1980) Pre-schoolers write messages and receive their favourite books, in *Language Arts*, 57, 7, 742–9, October.

LEICEISTERSHIRE SUPPORT SERVICE (undated) *Once Upon a Time . . . How children learn with Story Method.* Leicestershire LEA.

LOMAX, R. G. and MCGEE, L. M. (1987) Young children's concepts about print and reading: toward a model of word reading acqusition. *Reading Research Quarterly*, 22, 237–56.

MACKAY, D., THOMPSON, B., and SCHAUB, P. (1970) *Breakthrough to Literacy.* London: Longman.

MACDONALD, A. M. and KIRKPATRICK, E. M. (1980) *Chambers Everyday Dictionary.* W. & R. Chambers: Edinburgh.

MCGEE, L. M. (1986) Young Children's Environmental Print Reading, in *Childhood Education*, 63, 2, 118–25.

MEEK, M. (1982) *Learning to Read*, London: The Bodley Head.

MEEK, M. (1988) *How Texts Teach What Readers Learn.* Stroud, Glos: Thimble Press.

MICHAELS, S. (1980) *Sharing Time an Oral Preparation of Literacy.* Paper presented at the Ethnography in Educational Research Forum (University of Pennsylvania), Philadelphia.

MINNS, H. (1988) Teacher Inquiry in the Classroom: 'Read it to me now!' in *Language Arts*, 65, 4, 403–9.

MITCHELL, D. C. (1982) *The Process of Reading: A Cognitive Analysis of Fluent Reading and Learning to Read.* Chichester: Wiley.

MORRIS, J. (1989) Linguistics in a Lifetime of Learning about Language and Literacy in HUNTER-CARSCH, M. (ed.) *The Art of Reading.* Oxford: Basil Blackwell.

MORTIMORE, P., SAMMONS, P., STOLL, L. and ECOB, R. (1988) *School Matters – The Junior Years.* London: Open Books.

NATIONAL WRITING PROJECT (1985) Newsletter No. 1. London: SCDC Publications.

NATIONAL WRITING PROJECT (1988) Newsletter No. 10. London: SCDC Publications.

OAKHILL. J. and GARNHAM, A. (1988) *Becoming a Skilled Reader*. Oxford: Basil Blackwell.

ONIONS, C. T. (1965) *The Shorter Oxford English Dictionary*. Oxford: The Clarendon Press.

PATON, S. (1984) *Developing an Awareness of Print: A young child's first steps towards literacy*. Birmingham: Educational Review.

PERFETTI, C. A. (1985) *Reading Ability*. Oxford: Oxford University Press.

PETERS, R. S. (1969) *Perspectives on Plowden*. London: Routledge and Kegan Paul.

PETERS, M. (1970) *Success in Spelling: a study of the factors affecting improvement in spelling in the junior school*. Cambridge: Cambridge Institute of Education.

PLOWDEN REPORT (1967) *Children and their Primary Schools*. London: HMSO.

REID, J. (1972) Children's comprehension of syntactic features found in some extension readers. Occasional Paper, Centre for Research in Education Sciences, University of Edinburgh, in REID J. (ed.) *Reading Problems and Practices*. London: Ward Lock Educational.

RIST, R. (1970) Student social class and teacher expectations: the self-fulfilling prophesy in ghetto education, in *Harvard Educational Review* 40, 411–51.

ROUSSEAU, J. J. (1762) *Emile* (trans Barbara Foxley) London: Dent.

RUDDELL, R. B., (1965) The effect of oral and written patterns of language structure on reading comprehension, in *Reading Teacher*, 19, 270–5.

SMITH, F. (1988) *Joining the Literacy Club*. London. Heineman Educational Books.

SOUTHGATE, V., ARNOLD, H. and JOHNSON, S. (1981) *Extending Beginning Reading*. London: Heinemann.

STRICKLAND, R. (1962) The language of elementary school children: its relationship to the language of reading textbooks and the quality of reading of selected children, in *Bulletin of the School of Education*, Indiana University, 38 4, 1–131.

TIZARD, B. and HUGHES, M. (1988) *Young Children Learning: Talking and Thinking and Home and School*. London. Fontana.

TIZARD, B., BLATCHFORD, P., BURKE, J., FARQUHAR, C. and PLEWIS, I. (1988) *Young Children at School in the Inner City*. London. Lawrence Erlbaum Associates.

TIZARD, J., SCHOFIELD, W.N. and HEWISON, J. (1982) Collaboration between teachers and parents in assisting children's reading, *British Journal of Educational Psychology*, 52, 1–15.

TOUGH J. (1976) *Listening to Children Talking: a guide to the appraisal of children's language.* Communication Skills in Early Childhood. Schools' Council Project. London. Ward Lock Educational.

TUMNER, W. E. and BOWEY, J. A. (1984) Metalinguistic Awareness and Reading Acquisition, in W. E. TUMNER, C. PRATT and M. L. HERRIMAN (eds.) *Metalinguistic Awareness in Children: Theory Research and Implications.* Berlin: Springer-Verlag.

TWAY, E. (1983) When Will My Child Write? *Childhood Education*, 59, 5, 332–5.

UTAH INTER-INSTITUTIONAL SEMINAR IN CHILDHOOD EDUCATION (1978) Collected Papers 1978 Seminar. Weber State College, Ogden, Utah.

VAN DONGEN, R. D. (1979) Young Children Move into Reading supported by a classroom reading environment, *Insights into Open Education*, 2, 2, Videotape.

VYGOTSKY, L. (1962) *Thought and Language.* Cambridge, Mass. MIT.

VYGOTSKY, L. (1978) *Mind in Society: The Development of Higher Psychological Processes.* Cambridge, Mass. Harvard University Press.

WATERLAND, L. (1985) *Read With Me. An Apprenticeship Approach to Reading.* Stroud: Thimble Press.

WEBER, R. M. (1970) First Graders Use of Grammatical Context, in LEVIN, H. and WILLIAMS, J. P. (eds.) *Basic Studies in Reading.* New York: Basic Books Inc.

WELLS, C. G. (1981) *Learning Through Interaction.* Cambridge: Cambridge University Press.

WELLS, C. G. (1983) Talking with children: the complementary roles of parents and teachers, in DONALDSON, M., GRIEVE, R. and PRATT, C. (eds.) *Early Childhood Development and Education.* Oxford. Basil Blackwell.

WELLS, C. G. (1984) *Language Development in the Pre-School Years.* Cambridge: Cambridge University Press.

WELLS, C. G. (1987) *The Meaning Makers.* London: Hodder and Stoughton.

WOODWARD, V. A. (1988) Lessons from Eric: Talking and Writing about my Art, *Insights into Open Education*, 20, 8. Videotape.

YOUNG, G. (1988) Speech and Writing: the Development of a Model with a Functional Sentence Perspective, in HUNTER-CARSCH, M. (ed.) *The Art of Reading.* Oxford: Blackwell Education.

Book List

Children's books

AHLBERG, A. (1984) *Please Mrs Butler*. Puffin Books.
AHLBERG, A. and AHLBERG, J. (1986) *The Jolly Postman*. Heineman.
BAKER, J. (1987) *Where the Forest Meets the Sea*. Walker Books.
DAHL, R. (1985) *Charlie and the Chocolate Factory*. Allen and Unwin.
HUTCHINS, P. (1968) *Rosie's Walk*. Bodley Head.
MCKEE, D. (1980) *Not Now Bernard*. Anderson Press.
NICHOL, H. and PIENKOWSKI, J. (1975) *Meg and Mog*. Penguin.
WINTHROP, M. and DE PAOLA, T. (1988) *Maggie and the Monster*. Anderson Press.

Useful publications

Books for Keeps published by: The School Bookshop Association,
  1, Effingham Road,
  Lee,
  London SE12 8NZ.
The Good Book Guide to Children's Books. Yearly Editions by Penguin Books and Braithwaite and Taylor Ltd.